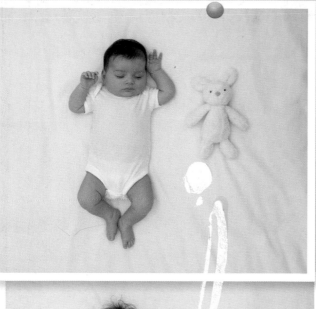

D0717384
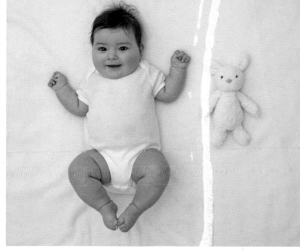

Watch My Baby Grow

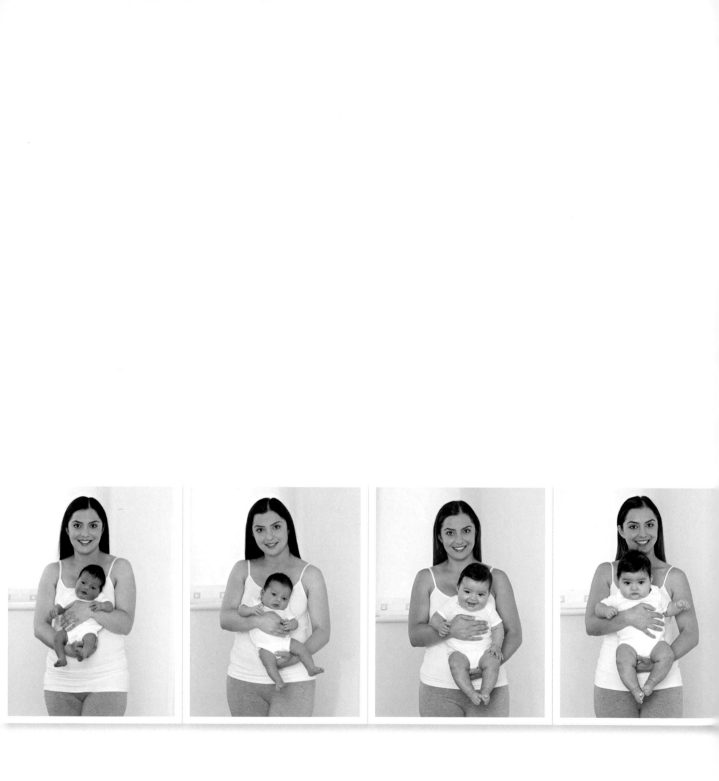

Watch My Baby Grow

Consultant Editor Susan Watt
Design and Photography Art Direction
Carole Ash at Project 360
Senior Editor Anne Hildyard
Project Editors Wendy Horobin, Jo Edwards,
Ann Baggaley
Senior Art Editor Jane Ewart
Project Art Editors Anne Fisher, Charlotte Johnson
Senior Jacket Creative Nicola Powling
Producer, Pre-Production Raymond Williams,
Rebecca Fallowfield
Producer Ché Creasey
Creative Technical Support Sonia Charbonnier
New Photography Ruth Jenkinson
Managing Editor Penny Smith
Managing Art Editor Marianne Markham
Publisher Mary Ling
Creative Director Jane Bull

First published in Great Britain in 2015
by Dorling Kindersley Limited,
80 Strand, London WC2R 0RL

A Penguin Random House Company
2 4 6 8 10 9 7 5 3 1
001–192949–Jan/2015
Copyright © 2015 Dorling Kindersley Limited
All rights reserved.

No part of this publication may be reproduced, stored in a
retrieval system, or transmitted in any form or by any means,
electronic, mechanical, photocopying, recording or otherwise,
without prior permission of the copyright owner.

A CIP catalogue record for this book
is available from the British Library.
ISBN 978-1-4093-6800-7

Printed and bound in China by Leo Paper Products Ltd.

A World of New Ideas
See All There Is To Know at
www.dk.com

*This book is dedicated to Melisa and
Helin, and their family. Without their
belief in the project, and their good-
natured and willing collaboration, this
book could not have been made.*

WREXHAM C.B.C LIBRARY LLYFRGELL B.S. WRECSAM	
C56 0000 0598 912	
Askews & Holts	03-Feb-2015
305.232	£16.99
ANF	CM

Contents

Introduction

If you've ever wanted to know what goes through a baby's head when she cries or smiles, this is the ideal book for you. It's all about helping mum, dad, carers, or grandparents to understand a baby's world, and gain an insight into what it's really like from her perspective. Although everyone knows a baby can make a powerfully affecting noise, does she feel anything, and what is really going on behind that frowning, intent gaze?

Until fairly recently, babies were considered to be cute, but not very aware. Now, however, it seems that their brains are perfectly capable of complex thought. The future is looking brighter for babies!

Once scientists became interested in finding out what makes babies tick, the age of the baby truly began. Innovative research projects produced some fascinating information: their studies, from many areas of science, reveal that babies are remarkable in their powers of learning, communication, and perception. Just like adults, they get to know things by experience, and can perform amazing feats almost as soon as they are born. They can recognize their mum's face and voice, learn to feed almost instantly, and they're eager to move their heads and hands. And they can influence those around them with their charm!

The idea for *Watch My Baby Grow* was conceived to discover what one baby was thinking and feeling at all stages of her development, right up until she was more than a year old.

This charming book stars an engaging baby, is written in an approachable, human way, and will appeal to anyone who is interested in a clear, scientific approach to every aspect of an infant's development.

One baby, one year,
one extraordinary project

Recording Melisa's First Year

Once upon a time, a DK book team had
a crazy plan to invade a family for the first year
of their baby's life – to take picture after
picture, and watch the baby grow.

They found the perfect fluffy rabbit to act
as the perfect measurer to show the baby's
growth. And then they found the perfect
pregnant someone, beautiful Seyhan…

*The toy rabbit, measuring
25.5 cm (10 in) from ears
to toes, was used as a height
guide throughout the year.*

Meet the team

More than 20 people helped to make this book. They include our consultant editor, our book designer and director of the photo shoots, the experts of Babylab at Birkbeck, University of London, the photographers, and, of course, the stars of the show – Melisa and her family.

WORKING TOGETHER FOR A YEAR forged a close working relationship within the team, which is reflected in the warm, intimate images that we managed to achieve. There were smiles and tears, but being involved with Melisa as she grew was a pleasure for all concerned.

Dr Victoria Southgate, Consultant at Birkbeck Babylab

Anna Durston, Hair and make-up artist

Ruth Jenkinson, Photographer

Susan Watt, Consultant editor

Carole Ash, Designer and shoot organiser

Helin   Seyhan   Melisa

Say cheese
Seyhan coaxes Melisa into drinking some more water for another shot.

Mobile Melisa
Now Melisa can move around, everything has to be baby-proofed for safety.

With a little help from mum, Melisa stands to look at the photographer.

Melisa attempts to crawl towards mum for a sequence of on-the-move shots.

On stage
Luckily the little star is very cooperative, and the team get the shots they want.

PHOTO-SHOOT LIST

During pregnancy:
- *Week 38*

After Melisa's birth:
- *Melisa on the same white background with rabbit, at two-, three-, and four-week intervals. Continue every four weeks until week 52.*

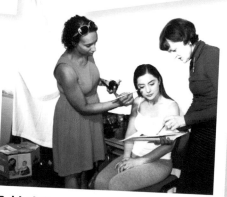

Behind the scenes
Seyhan looks at the plan for the day's shooting, while having her make-up applied.

Getting ready

Seyhan is two weeks into her maternity leave and can't wait to meet her baby. Mixed in with her excitement is a hint of trepidation about a photo-shoot team invading her home for the next year.

> *At the 20-week scan, Melisa looked like she was clapping her hands together. We like to think she was as excited as we were.*

PHOTO-SHOOT LIST

- Seyhan displaying her bump with various props & in poses that will be used in following shoot
- Bump & scan
- The happy parents
- Family shot

WHILE SEYHAN IS BUSY growing Melisa, the photo-shoot team are fully occupied planning all the shots that will showcase the baby's first year. Babies grow fast – they change both physically and mentally week by week. Meticulous planning is essential to ensure the team get every shot they need at every shoot, as there will be no chance of going back.

Week 1

Weight: 4.1kg (9lb)

A star is born – healthy, beautiful, and nine days late. Coping with both celebrations and sleep deprivation, it's a wonder Seyhan lets the photo team through the door.

PHOTO-SHOOT LIST
- Seyhan lying with Melisa
- Capture Melisa's expression after being fed

A MILK-DRUNK MELISA yawns contentedly following a feed. Like all newborn babies, Melisa has a tiny tummy that can't hold much milk, so she needs to feed often, at two-hourly intervals. At this stage, she'll sleep for up to 18 hours a day – but, unfortunately for Seyhan, just not 18 hours in a row.

Melisa was born with a full head of dark hair.

Week 3

Weight: 4.2 kg (9¼ lb)

Melisa is starting to adapt to the world and is getting to know her family. At this shoot, she has already begun to notice the photo-shoot team, and has everyone wrapped around her teeny-tiny finger.

THE WHITER-THAN-WHITE setting in each of these pictures, and the neutral colours throughout the shoot, ensure that nothing detracts from the star subject – baby Melisa. In this shot, a sleepy Melisa's unswaddled arms jump upwards as her "startle" reflex kicks in.

PHOTO-SHOOT LIST
- *Growth-chart shot*
- *Sequence of baby development shots, with close-ups of Melisa's hands, head & shoulders, & side view of head*

Most babies lose weight in the first week. Melisa is a good feeder and has steadily put on healthy weight from the start.

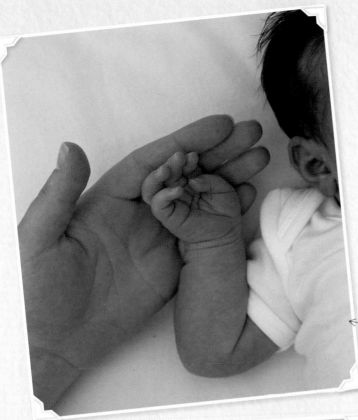

THE LITTLENESS OF Melisa's picture-perfect features and her exquisite petal-like hands are captured in this sequence of pictures. The lighting, positioning, and camera angles – all carefully recorded by the team – will be repeated at later stages in Melisa's first year to show her growth and development.

Melisa's flaky newborn nails were long when she was born, and she often scratched her soft skin.

AT THIS SHOOT, Melisa can focus only on things that are 25cm (10in) away from her. It was important to get a shot of Melisa with her eyes open so that any colour changes could be visually recorded. But Melisa is a very sleepy baby, and so capturing this called for some quick finger work by the photographer.

Curled-up sleep position

Milk blister on upper lip

Week 6

Weight: 4.8 kg (10½ lb)

Melisa continues to pack on healthy weight. She is starting to realize that her mum is extra special, so the photo shoot is interspersed with coos and kicks of pleasure whenever Seyhan interacts with her.

PHOTO-SHOOT LIST
- Seyhan holding baby
- Growth-chart shot
- Sequence of baby development shots, including close-ups of hands & feet

Toy rabbit placed in the same position at every shoot.

Melisa shows signs of tiredness.

THE TEAM LUCKED OUT with Melisa, who is a wonderfully calm baby – just perfect for the photo shoot. At six weeks, she is becoming sensitive to her surroundings, but in these early stages she generally stays in the position that she is put in. Here, a placid Melisa stretches in tiredness and closes her eyes during the growth-chart shots. Nap time is approaching – which also means a tea break for the team.

> *I enjoy being a part of the shoot, and I benefit from gaining some beautiful shots of my family.*

Seyhan holds up her daughter to show how Melisa is growing. Many later shoots will include similar photos for comparison.

Gummy-mouthed yawn

Soft, smooth skin

LOTS OF WET NAPPIES are a sign of a healthy baby, but some breastfed babies can go a week without passing faeces. This is because there is so little waste from breast milk. When the poo does come though, it just keeps on coming. This shot was taken seconds before Melisa had one of those moments. Needless to say, every item of clothing was ruined.

Week 8

Weight: 5.9 kg (13 lb)

Melisa no longer looks like a newborn at this shoot. The wrinkly skin has filled out and she has changed into a roly-poly baby who is suddenly aware that her arms and legs belong to her.

PHOTO-SHOOT LIST
- Melisa's hand in Seyhan's
- Melisa focusing on toy & sticking her tongue out
- Melisa doing tummy time
- Melisa & Helin interacting

" Melisa all of a sudden seems so big – it is as if she has grown overnight. "

Helin loves any opportunity for baby cuddles.

WHEN PRESENTED WITH A TOY, Melisa can focus on it and track its movement from side to side. Her eye coordination is still developing, so she often appears cross-eyed when she tries to focus – something her sister Helin finds hilarious. Now that she is aware of her limbs, Melisa reaches out and grabs at toys, too, making that growth-chart shot a little more tricky.

Getting stronger at tummy time

Melisa can see and reach for toys, and have a little game of tug-of-war, too.

Melisa spends most of her time on her back.

Week 12

Weight: 6.5 kg (14 lb)

PHOTO-SHOOT LIST

- *Seyhan holding Melisa*
- *Overhead view of Melisa to chart her growth*
- *Close-up of Melisa using her hands*
- *Facial development*

At three months of age, most babies show clear signs of their character. Melisa is starting to reveal her sense of humour, flashing gummy smiles that disarm everyone in the room.

MELISA'S HAND–EYE COORDINATION is developing rapidly. As well as showing off her increasing dexterity by sucking her thumb, she grasps at a toy that is held out to her, and loves lying under her play gym to swat at the toys dangling above her.

> " *Melisa likes to suck her thumb, but she misses and hits each part of her face before finding her mouth.* "

Face creases when crying

Smiles for mum

BY THE TIME they are three months old, most babies can hold their head steady for longer, and turn to the sound of their mother's voice. They can make smooth movements of limbs and may be able to lift the head and shoulders when lying flat.

Week 16

Weight: 7.3 kg (16 lb)

Babies love to play and to be held, and Melisa squeals with delight during these interactive shots with Seyhan. Her laugh draws smiles from the whole team.

MELISA'S PHYSICAL STRENGTH has been clear from the start. Within the first few weeks she developed strong neck muscles, which helped keep her heavy head steady without support. She has enjoyed lots of tummy time, too, lifting her head to gaze around her. There is no doubt that playtime with Mum is her favourite way of exercising mind and body.

PHOTO-SHOOT LIST

• *Seyhan & Melisa making eye contact with each other*

• *Melisa responding to Seyhan with smiles*

• *Melisa engaging with a toy*

• *Melisa showing increased strength during tummy time with her head lifted up*

Strong neck muscles

Responding to Mum's smiles

MELISA'S THOUGHTFUL GAZES when presented with toys show that she is starting to make sense of the world around her. Her mental development is helped along by her physical strength as she learns to control and manipulate her upper body, and engages more fully with people and toys.

Melisa was always a strong baby. I didn't have to worry much about holding her head.

Melisa loves this toy with a rattle inside.

Teething signs
Melisa started teething at about three to four months – cue lots of dribble. Because of this, the photo shoot often had to be stopped to change Melisa's babygros, which quickly became soaked through.

Week 20
Weight: 7.8 kg (17 lb)

With the fine-tuning of her senses almost complete, a whole new sensory world has opened up to Melisa. She is now interested in anything and everything.

IT TAKES SEYHAN FOREVER to dress, feed, and nappy-change her baby, as Melisa is so easily distracted by her surroundings. An extra pair of hands always comes in useful for holding the little wriggler. Happily sitting in Seyhan's arms one minute, she suddenly flings herself backwards and exerts every scrap of strength to look in the opposite direction. And if she can't reach what she wants, she becomes increasingly frustrated.

MELISA LOVES big sister, Helin, who is almost four years old. With a new awareness of the activity and noises around her, Melisa soon realized that here was another special, smiley, very funny person in her life. Most babies of this age anticipate something funny as they recognize repeated sounds, and Helin's rendition of "Wind the bobbin up" with hand actions makes Melisa laugh a lot.

" Just seeing Helin every morning brings the biggest smile to Melisa's face. Whatever Helin does, Melisa loves. "

PHOTO-SHOOT LIST

- Melisa & Helin interacting
- Melisa responding to Helin & Seyhan
- Seyhan holding Melisa

Hunt the toy
Toys are no longer "out of sight, out of mind". Melisa follows and searches for a toy, even if it drops to the floor and is out of her line of vision.

Week 24

Weight: 8.3 kg (18¼ lb)

Melisa is developing rapidly, her core and limb muscles growing stronger by the day. With more refined coordination, she can reach out and grab things – including forbidden "toys", such as earrings.

HELIN IS ALWAYS at the shoots, an adoring and attentive big sister. "Although she was adamant she wanted a brother, she soon admitted that having a sister was pretty cool," Seyhan laughs. Far from being camera shy, Helin wants to be in the shots, and the photo-shoot team are happy to oblige. For this picture, Helin proved a more malleable model than her sister. Despite the photographer's keen attempts to get Melisa's attention, Melisa is focused on something in the other direction and will not be deterred.

> **Melisa is at the stage where she grabs everything, including my hair, and won't let go.**

PHOTO-SHOOT LIST

- Family shot with Helin & Seyhan
- Melisa laughing & interacting with Seyhan

MOBILE TOYS, dangly earrings, long hair – all attract a swipe and grab from six-month-old Melisa. Babies of this age can usually bring their hands together to grasp things. Like other babies in their first year, Melisa favours a particular hand at times, but changes it from month to month.

PHOTO-SHOOT LIST

• Baby development shots: hands grasping at toy, close-up of feet to show plantar reflex

Pointed toes

Happy smiles for mum

Plantar reflex
Melisa points her toes a lot. This ballerina impersonation is the result of the plantar reflex – when the sole of the foot is stroked, her foot flexes and the toes curl.

Week 28

Weight: 8.7 kg (19 lb)

Because Melisa has acquired such an impressive collection of toys, the photo-shoot team is running out of space to work in the family's home. A change in location to a nearby church hall is necessary.

PHOTO-SHOOT LIST

• *Series of shots to show Melisa's coordination & sensory development*

MUCH TO SEYHAN'S DELIGHT, Melisa loves books. She anticipates the repetitive sounds of her mum's voice reading a favourite story and, not yet able to discern between 2D and 3D, she grabs at the colourful pictures. Predictably, Melisa also does her best to chew the book.

Colourful pictures attract Melisa's attention.

WITH SEYHAN SUPPORTING HER, Melisa is able to stand, building up strength in her legs to walk. The ecstatic excitement on her face and cute coos show that she knows she is doing something clever. Sometimes, she bends her knees and bounces, exercising her legs and core musles, and giving Seyhan an upper arm workout, too.

Baby steps
Her instinct to walk is strong. A very wobbly Melisa tentatively moves one foot forward.

Getting the message across
Melisa is now able to make it perfectly clear whether she is happy, or sad, or frustrated. Here, she is complaining about a toy being taken away.

Melisa turns towards any unfamiliar noise.

PHOTO-SHOOT LIST

- Play & interaction between Melisa & Seyhan
- Melisa standing with support
- Growth-chart shot

What's that sound?
Melisa is used to the sound of the camera taking shots, but turns towards any new sound.

Week 32
Weight: 9.2 kg (20¼ lb)

PHOTO-SHOOT LIST
- Melisa showing increased coordination & engagement in play
- Melisa exploring things with her mouth

In this photo shoot, Melisa uses her hands a lot. She reaches for toys, points with her fists, grabs, holds, and bangs with her hands. She also tries exploring things with her mouth.

CAPTIVATED BY ANYTHING NEW, Melisa sits and observes when Helin reads her a peekaboo book. She cannot resist launching herself forward to rustle the scrunchy fabric and lift the tabs to find what is underneath.

Peekaboo!
The anticipation behind this game has Melisa giggling before you can even say "peekaboo!"

New tastes
Like all babies, Melisa puts everything in her mouth. Since she started on solids a few weeks ago, she is progressing naturally to trying to feed herself.

Clapping encouragement

Applause
Now more socially aware and able to interact, Melisa repeats an action whenever she is rewarded with a round of applause.

Exploring with mouth

SITTING UP UNAIDED, a playful Melisa wants to explore everything. When presented with a colourful new toy, she can't wait to get her hands on it. Typical of her age group, she first shakes it, bangs it, and drops it to see what happens. Then she puts it in her mouth – which has more nerve endings than any other part of her body – for the tried-and-tested mouthing method of further exploration.

Week 36

Weight: 9.4 kg (20¾ lb)

Getting Melisa to sit still for a picture has become a mammoth challenge, now she's on the move with a bottom-shuffle crawl. Her dad, Ulas, and her granny agree to be a part of the photo-shoot action, and to run around after Melisa.

> " One day, Ulas and I were talking about Melisa. I said her name and her head spun round. Just like that, she knew her name. "

PHOTO-SHOOT LIST

- Family group: Seyhan & Ulas playng with the children

PHOTO-SHOOT LIST

• Granny with Melisa, to show family resemblance & interaction between generations

NOW NINE MONTHS OLD, Melisa has started to crawl. Well, her version of crawling that is…. Many babies begin with a traditional on-all-fours crawl, but Melisa shuns this method and bottom-shuffles her way around, one leg curled beneath her and her arms doing most of the work. Once babies are more mobile and can increase the distance between themselves and their mummies, separation anxiety often sets in. One way to reduce the effect of this is to leave children with their grandparents on a regular basis, so that they get used to "other people". Living just around the corner, Seyhan's mum loves looking after her grandchildren, and the two girls love having granny as their nanny.

Learning two languages
Melisa's family are bilingual, speaking Turkish at home, and English elsewhere. Melisa and Helin's granny speaks only Turkish to the two girls. Following her example, Helin speaks only Turkish to Melisa. She was heard telling Melisa not to worry – she would learn English at nursery.

Week 40

Weight: 9.7 kg (21 ¼ lb)

Strong and supple, Melisa is constantly moving around, exploring everything. Getting her to sit still for shots requires lots of new toys, funny faces, and raspberry blowing.

A HIGHLY MOBILE MELISA lies on her back just long enough for the growth-chart shot, mesmerized for a few seconds by the photographer's funny noises. At playtime, she's beginning to experiment – not yet able to stack blocks, but very much into tower demolition, and thrilled with each new accomplishment.

PHOTO-SHOOT LIST

- Series of shots to show Melisa's increasing mobility & improving balance
- Growth-chart shot
- Melisa playing with toys

Starting to recognize order with stacked rings.

Never still
Any opportunity to play with her feet and put them in her mouth is seized by Melisa.

Swimming actions
Melisa makes swimming motions when she's on her tummy, wanting to be on the move the whole time.

Strong core muscles

> **Melisa's balance has improved so much since her first standing shot, at week 28. She was very wobbly then!**

EXCITED BY THE DIFFERENT VIEW from her standing height, Melisa is getting better at keeping her balance when helped to an upright position. Here, propped confidently against her little table, she's on the lookout for that toy she remembers being taken away and stashed behind a box just over there…

Getting balanced

Week 44

Weight: 10.1 kg (22½ lb)

With three solid meals on top of milk feeds, lots of crawling, exploring, and playing, as well as two naps, Melisa's day is a full one. And that's without a photo shoot to boot.

PHOTO-SHOOT LIST

- *Melisa feeding, showing how she grasps her spoon & tries to feed herself*
- *Series of shots to show Melisa's facial expressions*

BABIES ARE BORN with enough iron to supply their little bodies for the first six months of life. From then on, they need a source of food other than their mother's milk to help boost this supply. Melisa began this new regime just before she was six months, with iron-fortified rice cereal, plus puréed fruit and vegetables. Sweet potato, pumpkin, and all fruits are clear winners with Melisa, who grabs at the spoon if it's something she likes in a messy attempt to feed herself. Efforts to keep food out of Melisa's hands and save the white background sheet at this photo shoot were an epic failure.

> *Melisa is a good eater and loves all her food. But she definitely opens her mouth wider for something sweet.*

Enough's enough

The photo shoot is over and Melisa shows signs of weariness – yawning, pulling her ear, rubbing her eyes, and sucking her thumb.

Expressive looks

Melisa reveals a lot about how she feels with her facial expressions as she continues to develop socially. Enraptured by Helin, she watches her intently and looks to her to share something funny.

OTHERWISE A SOCIABLE BABY, if Melisa is teething, tired or just out of sorts, she becomes shy and uncertain, sucking her thumb to self-soothe but needing reassuring cuddles from mum, too. After dropping a nap from her routine, she is now very sleepy at the end of the day.

Week 48

Weight: 10.4 kg (23 lb)

This shoot explores Melisa's repertoire of skills, and her experiments with tastes and textures. She doesn't always come up with the reactions everyone expected.

PARTICULAR WORDS grab Melisa's attention as she begins to understand and associate them with objects and actions. She is becoming her own person, asserting herself with sister Helin at times, and playing alongside her ("parallel play") at others. She still checks her mum's response to things she is uncertain about, though.

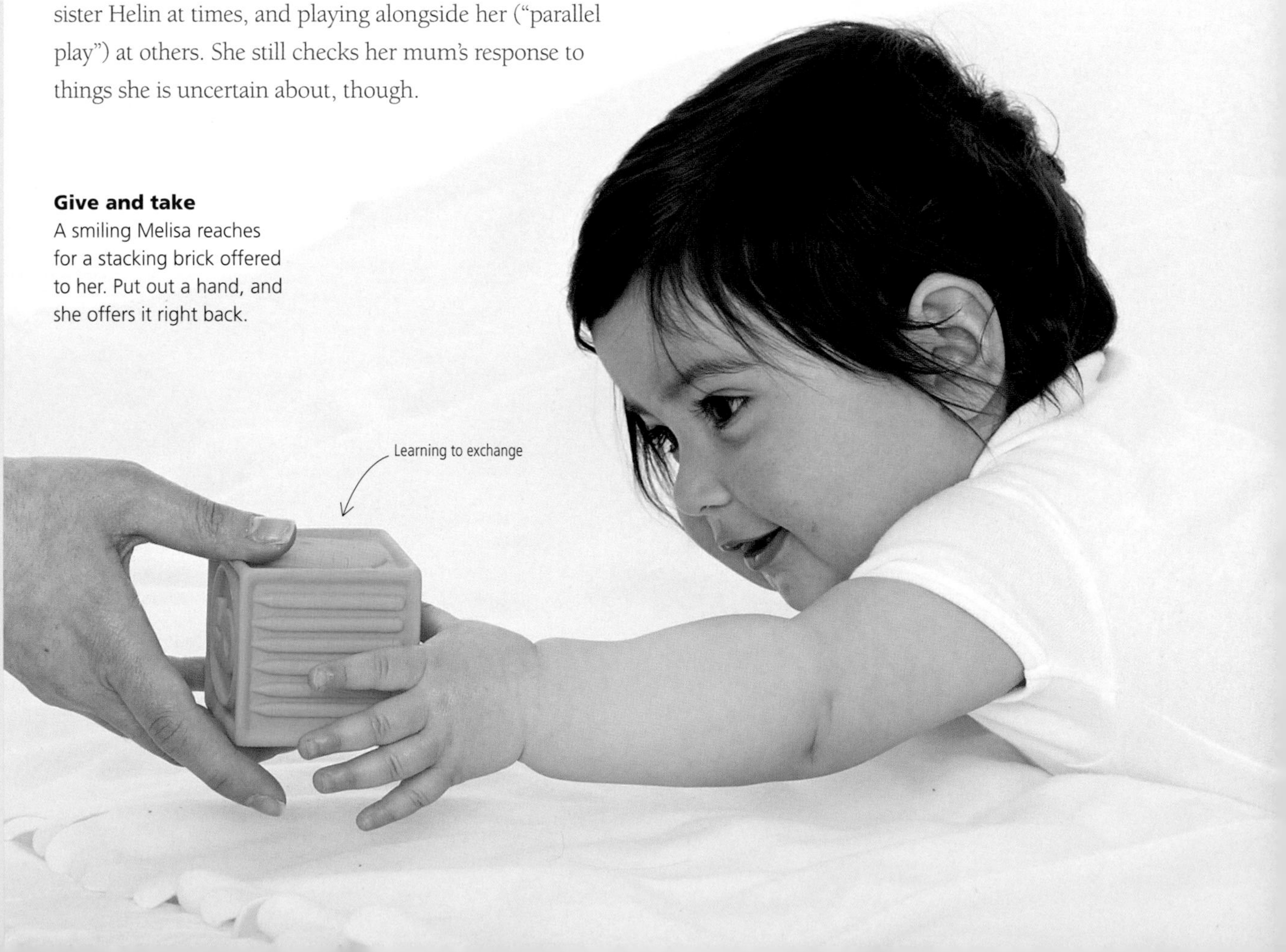

PHOTO-SHOOT LIST

- Melisa reacting to sounds & words
- Melisa experimenting with different textures
- Melisa reacting to different tastes

Give and take
A smiling Melisa reaches for a stacking brick offered to her. Put out a hand, and she offers it right back.

Learning to exchange

Feels funny
The rough bristles of a brush are a new texture for Melisa, and she is not sure she really likes it.

Touch and smell
Melisa is a big fan of leaves in the park, and finds this basil plant, with its soft texture and aromatic smell, a sensory treat.

Interesting toes
If there's nothing else to touch and explore, Melisa finds her toes a good alternative.

Missing the beat
Melisa has learned to wave her arms in time to the beat rattled out by the maraca – she just doesn't want to at this shoot.

Unexpected reaction
Far from finding a lemon too sour, Melisa loved the taste. Her expression of enjoyment surprised everyone.

Week 52
Weight: 10.5 kg (23 ¼ lb)

Unaware that it is her birthday, but loving the fuss, Melisa is one year old. This huge milestone marks both the end of the photo shoots, and the start of a new year that will see Melisa walking and talking.

AT THIS AGE, babies maintain their insatiable desire to explore and are growing in independence. With every new mastered skill, from standing and walking to feeding herself, Melisa steps further away from helpless babyhood and is becoming a little lady.

Look and learn
While Helin plays, Melisa watches, listens, and then copies, keen to get involved in the birthday fun.

PHOTO-SHOOT LIST

- Melisa learning how to party by copying sister Helin
- Birthday fun & treats
- Melisa's progress with standing, holding on to her mum

WITH HER FINE MOTOR SKILLS mastered, Melisa is making more use of her larger muscles, pulling up to standing. Of course, she has the occasional tumble and still needs a little help from mum, but her confidence is growing. Sadly our photo team won't be around to capture the ongoing moments of Melisa's little achievements. She hasn't quite learnt to walk yet, but with her burgeoning strength and coordination it won't be long. The sadness of bidding farewell to this happy family is mitigated by the great privilege we have enjoyed in being able to watch their baby grow.

Hasn't she grown!

At regular intervals during the year, Melisa was photographed with her toy rabbit, who looks smaller each time!

WEEK 1

WEEK 3

WEEK 6

WEEK 8

WEEK 12

WEEK 32

WEEK 36

WEEK 40

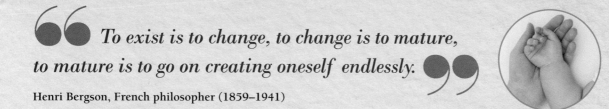

> *To exist is to change, to change is to mature,*
> *to mature is to go on creating oneself endlessly.*

Henri Bergson, French philosopher (1859–1941)

WEEK *16*

WEEK *20*

WEEK *24*

WEEK *28*

WEEK *44*

WEEK *48*

WEEK *52*

Newborn

Before...

EVERYONE IS EXCITED about the impending birth. Big sister Helin likes to feel the baby move and kick. And baby, although not yet born, is already familiar with the sounds and rhythms of life around her. She will know mum's voice and perhaps her big sister's, too, if she has heard it enough.

After...

FOLLOWING A SPEEDY delivery, the baby has finally made her eagerly anticipated appearance. Melisa weighs 4.1kg (9lb) – that's big! – and, like her sister when she was born, she has a full head of hair. Her rosy red colour is a sign that she is robustly healthy – so now it's all systems go! She is already fascinated by voices and can recognize when familiar people, like her mum and sister, are talking to her.

Newborn baby reflexes

Babies are born with a set of automatic, unconscious reflexes, a gift from our evolutionary past. Some of these are no longer useful – but they are all there for a reason.

NEWBORN BABIES have so little control over their movements, it's a wonder that they are able to survive at all. Yet humans have evolved so they are born with a large collection of instinctive reflexes – about 70 in total – which work automatically in the right situation. Many of these can be traced to our primate ancestors, when their function was crucial for survival.

Reflexes help protect and guide a baby in those first months outside the womb, and they serve a variety of functions. Some, for example, ensure that a baby is ready to feed as soon as she is born, others are intended for self-protection. As the brain develops, these reflexes give way to more deliberate behaviours, and their disappearance is an important sign that the baby's brain is developing properly.

{ A baby's instinctive reflexes change to deliberate behaviours in the first six months. }

ROOT REFLEX

Within the first hour of birth, if a baby feels a touch on the side of her cheek she will turn her head and "root" in that direction. This ensures she can find mum's breast or the teat of a bottle. Yet scientists argue over whether rooting should in fact be considered a reflex, as it seems to be under a degree of conscious control. Rooting is less likely to happen if the baby is not hungry, or if she touches her own cheek, both of which suggest it is not as involuntary as other reflexes.

SUCK REFLEX

The rooting reflex prepares the baby to suck – when the roof of the mouth is touched the baby will begin sucking furiously. This reflex is not fully developed until the 36th week of pregnancy, which is why premature babies may have trouble feeding. The suck reflex primarily ensures that a newborn will instinctively eat, but sucking is also a key source of comfort for a baby.

HAND TO MOUTH REFLEX

While rooting and sucking are the most well-known feeding reflexes, another is the "hand to mouth" reflex. This is when a baby flexes her arm and brings her hand up to her mouth in response to a stroke on the palm of her hand or her cheek – she then sucks on her fingers. Initially, she lacks the strength to keep her hand in place for long, so the reflex remains until she is able to make this action consciously, and suck on her fingers when she feels the need.

GRASP REFLEX

If you put your finger in the palm of a newborn baby, she will grasp it tightly – a reaction known as the "palmar grasp" reflex. This reflex response is a throwback to our primate ancestors whose babies used it to cling to their mother's fur as she moved around. The grasp

FIRST RESPONSES A newborn's reflexes are all in place at birth, and the most familiar of these relate to feeding and self-protection. As the baby grows and develops, the need for a reflex disappears and the action gradually fades – either in a matter of weeks or months.

SUCK AND ROOT

A baby roots and then sucks in response to anything that stimulates the mouth; usually lasts about three or four months.

GRASP

A baby grips whatever is placed in her palm; usually lasts about two months.

HAND TO MOUTH

A baby brings her hand to her mouth to suck; usually lasts until about four months.

TONIC NECK

When the arm and head move in the same direction; usually lasts five to seven months.

STARTLE

The baby flings her arms up in response to feeling like she's falling; usually lasts about two months.

DIVE

When a baby's windpipe closes in response to contact with water; usually lasts until about six months.

STEP

When a baby's feet and legs move in a "stepping" motion; usually lasts about two months.

A baby is born with about 70 instinctive reflexes

reflex is also present in newborn babies' feet, and this is another link to our evolutionary past, as baby monkeys cling with both their hands and feet.

STARTLE REFLEX

If a baby feels as if she is falling, or she hears a loud noise, she will throw up her arms as if she is trying to grab onto something – a dramatic action called the "startle", or "Moro" reflex. As with the grasp reflex, this stems from a baby's primitive instinct to hold on and save herself. Babies can also experience a startle reflex when dropping off to sleep, so some parents swaddle their newborn to prevent her from waking herself up.

STEP REFLEX

When a newborn baby is held upright and feels a surface beneath her feet, she starts to move her legs as though she was walking. Although this "step" reflex seems to disappear at around two months, scientists have shown that if you place an older baby

> … this "step" reflex seems to disappear… if you place a baby waist-deep in water, the reflex is still present.

waist-deep in a tank of water (so that she feels weightless), the step reflex is still present. The reason they stop stepping is because accumulating baby fat makes it quite an effort to lift those little legs! The stepping reflex might also have other uses: before birth, babies use their legs to brace themselves against the wall of the womb and turn around; after birth, the step reflex helps the baby to push against mum during feeding and keep herself in the correct position.

TONIC NECK REFLEX

A baby lying on her back often turns her head to the side (usually to the right) and extends her arm in the same direction. This action – the "tonic neck" reflex – needs to disappear so that the baby can learn to roll over. In the meantime, it might protect newborns from rolling on to their tummies before they can lift their heads up properly. Scientists have speculated that babies' preference for turning their head to the right is related to becoming right-handed later on.

Feed me Babies perform the hand to mouth reflex automatically when their hand or cheek is stroked. Sucking on their fingers brings them comfort, but babies do this consciously themselves only when they are a few months old.

On guard! The tonic neck reflex is also known – aptly – as the "fencing posture", as shown above. This reflex also enables a baby to observe her hands, which gives her crucial information about her own movements.

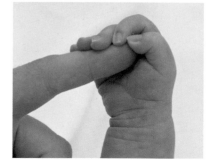

Little monkey A baby's grasp reflex is so instinctive that one of the hardest things for a newborn to do is let go! It is even claimed that a newborn can support her own weight if left to hang from a washing line – but don't try this!

❝ *Reflexes help protect and guide a baby in those first months outside the womb, and they serve a variety of functions.* **❞**

HICCUP!

All mammals, young or old, hiccup, but newborns hiccup most, and by some estimates spend 2.5 per cent of their time hiccuping! One theory is that the hiccup evolved to remove air from the stomach of nursing babies, but serves little function in adults. Feeding babies need to suck and breathe at the same time, and, as a result, can end up swallowing air. Hiccuping removes the air, making room for nutritious milk.

WATER BABIES

Newborns have a remarkable ability to survive in water. If they are submerged, not only can they propel themselves forward, but the windpipe closes off so any water taken in goes into the stomach instead of the lungs. This "dive" reflex is shared with many other mammals and may be a clue to our reptilian past. Some scientists, however, think the dive reflex is an adaptation from living in amniotic fluid for nine months – something that other mammals do, too. Even if we can't be certain about the origins of this reflex, it is the reason behind the miraculous survival of some babies who have accidentally fallen into water.

Pool champions Until about six months, babies put in water, front-side down, will move their arms and legs to look as if they are actually swimming.

Knowing where mum is is vital for a newborn's sense of security. Newborn babies need their mum for everything, from food to warmth. They quickly learn to sense her through sound, smell, and touch. And even though their vision is poor at first, they'll soon learn to recognize her face by sight, too.

That's my mum

Although a newborn baby has never seen her mother before, she already knows the sound of her voice. After birth, she will learn to recognize her with all her senses, and they will share a lifelong bond.

THE BOND THAT DEVELOPS between a baby and her mother in the first hours, days, and months after birth is as important for the baby's physical health as it is for her emotional wellbeing.

From the moment of birth, a baby is exposed to a multitude of new sensations, many of which will feel stressful to a newborn. For tiny babies, being close to their mother is the most important way to manage this stress. Her voice, her face, her smell, and her touch provide all that a newborn baby needs to cope with these new experiences. These early lessons in stress management may even inform the way in which the newborn's hormone-controlling genes respond to future stressful events.

No wonder then that nature has ensured that newborn babies are primed to learn how to quickly recognize their mother, and to take special comfort in her reassuring touch and hearing her soothing voice.

MUM'S VOICE

During the third trimester, babies begin to hear their mum's voice from within the womb, and the process of forming a relationship starts then. If a newborn baby hears a recording of mum's voice, her heart starts to beat faster. Scientists have also shown that newborns will suck harder on a pacifier if they can hear their mum's voice, rather than a stranger's voice. Some doctors have even begun to use this fact to encourage premature babies to practice sucking, and improve their ability to feed. Newborn babies can detect their mum's voice even while they are sleeping, and mum's voice may also have a special role to play in language learning. During one study, when scientists looked at the brains of sleeping newborns, they found that only the mother's voice was able to activate the language area of the brain.

> The distance between the baby and her mum's face during breastfeeding is … the optimal distance for newborn vision.

MUM'S FACE

While a newborn has never seen her mother before, it takes only a matter of hours for her to begin to recognize her mum's face and choose to look at her rather than another female face.

Newborns cannot see very clearly at first, yet they can detect enough to recognize the important features of the face, such as the eyes and mouth. The distance between the baby and her mum's face during breastfeeding is actually the optimal distance for newborn vision – about 30cm (12in).

Nevertheless, even though they can make out the features of mum's face, newborn babies actually rely more on the outline features, like head shape and hairline, to recognize their mum.

> *Being skin-to-skin with mum helps to regulate the baby's heartbeat and breathing rhythms… Close physical contact also leads to the release of oxytocin (the "love" hormone) in both mum and baby, which kicks off the bonding process…*

BABY FACTS

Most babies prefer to look at female faces, although babies who are raised by their father prefer to look at male faces. From a few months old, babies also prefer gazing at faces that resemble people close to them.

MUM'S SCENT

A sense of smell is an especially powerful tool for learning in newborn babies, and they are rapidly able to recognize the smell of their mother's skin and her breast milk. Research suggests that babies who experience an hour of skin-to-skin contact immediately after birth learn to recognize their mother's milk better than infants who do not have skin-to-skin contact immediately. Mum's smell has a clever, calming effect on newborns, creating a relaxed, nurturing environment.

MUM'S MILK

Newborns who are having a routine heel-prick blood test have been found to cry less and have lower levels of stress hormones if they can smell mum's milk. This soothing effect of mum's smell is why many sleep experts recommend putting babies to sleep on a t-shirt that mum has been wearing.

MUM'S SKIN

The feeling of the baby's skin on mum's skin is important for physical and emotional reasons. Newborn babies can't regulate their own body temperature yet, but the feeling of the baby on mum's chest makes her own body temperature change in order to keep the baby at the perfect temperature. Being skin-to-skin with mum helps to regulate the baby's heartbeat and breathing rhythms. This close physical contact also leads to the release of oxytocin (the "love" hormone) in both mum and baby, which helps kicks off the bonding process.

Newborns can detect the smell of their mother's breast milk from a distance of about 17cm (6¹/₂in), and will try to get closer to this smell.

How babies bond

Parents inevitably fall in love with their new babies. While the ease with which this happens may make us take it for granted, bonding relies on a whole range of brain and behavioural processes to get going.

ALTHOUGH IT MAY NOT always be instantaneous, the bonding process comes naturally to most newborns and their mums and dads. Unknown to both baby and parent, their brains have been preparing for this relationship since before birth, building up levels of a bonding hormone called oxytocin, and getting their biological clocks tuned in to tap into each other's rhythms.

TUNING IN

From the moment of birth, newborns and their parents unwittingly begin to synchronize their behaviour. Parents naturally gaze into their babies' eyes and talk to them in high-pitched baby-talk. When they do this, their babies become more alert – and this makes parents talk even more! At the same time, newborns have clever ways of initiating these periods of coordination, too. Rather than sucking continuously, a breastfeeding newborn will suck in bursts. In those moments when they pause, mums will gently rock their babies until they start sucking again – a very simple illustration of how both the baby and mum work together.

KEEPING TIME

The human biological clock, which tells us when to sleep and when to wake, and which controls our heartbeat, might also be crucial for getting babies in sync with their mums. This inner timekeeping is controlled by cells located in the hypothalamus in the brain, and develops during the third trimester of pregnancy. In this way, a baby's brain gets ready for being able to keep time with her mum while she is still in the womb. Babies whose biological clocks mature earlier have been found to take part in more synchronous behaviour with their mum in the first months outside the womb.

> Babies whose biological clocks mature earlier … take part in more synchronous behaviour

CHEMICAL REACTIONS

When parents talk about falling in love with their newborn baby, it's no exaggeration. Oxytocin, the feel-good hormone released when we experience romantic love, is also responsible for forging the bond between a newborn and her parents.

For both Mum and Dad, oxytocin levels start to rise during pregnancy, and higher levels of oxytocin are related to more synchronous behaviour with their baby, and hence, better bonding.

Although oxytocin is often associated with birth and breastfeeding, touch is also an important trigger for oxytocin release, and dads who engage in lots of contact with their babies release just as much oxytocin as mums. For mums, oxytocin is released primarily after periods of chatting and cuddling with their baby, while for dads it is triggered by activities, such as showing the baby new things or a game of rough-and-tumble.

Seeing a picture of her newborn baby activates the same areas of a woman's brain that are involved in drug addiction, suggesting that the same kind of "high" happens simply by a mum looking at her brand new baby.

Not only do mums and babies synchronize their behaviour, but also their hearts, which will slow down or speed up in time with one another. While most mammals require touch in order for their hearts to synchronize, human mums and babies can achieve this just by looking at each other.

Mums and babies can synchronize their heart beats just by looking at each other.

Although lots of factors probably influence IQ, the quality of mum and baby synchrony in the first year of life seems to be one of these. Babies who experience more synchrony with their mums seem to have a higher IQ.

Hearing their newborn baby cry changes brain activity in mums but not in dads – perhaps this is the reason why mums seem to find it harder to ignore their babies' cries!

Help me!

When babies are born, they are completely helpless and need their parents to do almost everything for them. However, there are good reasons why babies are born this way.

ALTHOUGH BABIES ARE BORN with heads that seem oversized, the brain inside is decidedly underpowered – and still only 25 per cent of its adult size. The brain of a newborn baby is very immature, and it will be many months before she is even able to control her own movements. So, why are babies born in a helpless state, dependent on others for several months?

WHEN TO COME OUT?

For a long time, anthropologists believed the main reason for a newborn's immaturity was the constraints of the birth process itself: babies need to be born before their heads become too large for the birth canal, leaving little time for the brain to develop. Why, then, did humans not simply evolve with a wider birth canal to make the process easier? The reason was thought to be that humans need a narrower pelvis than other primates because we walk upright. To walk, we need to be able to stand momentarily on one leg – which is only possible

{ A chimpanzee is born with a brain 40% of its adult size; a human baby's brain is 25% of adult size. }

if our weight is positioned fairly centrally, over a narrow pelvis. Indeed, no other primate is able to do this comfortably. While a narrow pelvis facilitates upright walking, it is less useful for childbirth.

But scientists now think there may be an even more important reason why babies are born comparatively early: the size of baby that a mother can support in her womb is limited by the demands on the mother herself. After six months of pregnancy, the mother's body is working at twice its normal metabolic rate to provide sufficient energy to grow and maintain new cells in the baby, and by nine months it has reached its limit – so the baby is born.

WHO'S AT THE CONTROLS?

Newborn babies are unable to control their movements, choose what they want to look at, or regulate their emotions. They depend completely on others to move them out of harm's way, or calm them down when they are upset. The reason for this

HEAD AND BRAIN SIZE

At birth, a baby's actual head is disproportionately large, making up about one-third of its total body length. Yet the brain itself is still just one quarter of the size it will reach by adulthood, and as such is very underdeveloped. However, during the first few weeks and months, a baby's brain continues to grow incredibly fast in response to new experiences: a five year old's brain is 90 per cent of its adult size.

AT BIRTH

The brain is **25%** of its adult size.

1 YEAR

Increases rapidly to **60%** of adult size.

18 YEARS

The brain continues to grow into adulthood.

Extra carers, such as grandparents and other relatives, can help by looking after the dependent newborn baby.

helplessness is largely because the frontal cortex of the brain – which acts as the "command centre" – is underdeveloped at birth. This region, located just behind the forehead, matures slowly through infancy, childhood, and adolescence, and is only fully developed by adulthood.

However, newborn helplessness has a flip side. The baby doesn't need to worry about taking care of herself, and can concentrate on learning about the world at her own pace. Also, the brain can develop in a way that fits the baby's environment. Rather than depend on set behaviours and simple responses, human babies can learn in a flexible, creative way.

HELPLESS BABIES, CARING PARENTS

When it comes to bringing up a newborn, many cultures adopt a "divide and conquer" strategy where a whole family helps to care for the baby – for example in Africa, where the proverb "it takes a village to raise a child" originated. In Western societies, nannies and kindergartens often help to look after infants.

BRAIN DEVELOPMENT AND CONNECTIONS

A newborn's brain has most of its neurons (brain cells), with just a few connections (synapses) between them. These allow it to carry out basic functions. Further connections form rapidly as the brain receives stimulation, linking areas of the brain to develop new abilities, such as speech or face recognition. Connections either strengthen and remain, or fade away if they are underused.

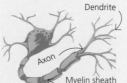

Neuron (brain cell)
Dendrite
Axon
Myelin sheath

Neural network at one year.

Neural network in adult brain.

Making connections

A newborn baby's brain is ready for essential functions, but it is really just starting to develop.

EVERY BABY IS BORN with most of the brain cells it will ever have – about one hundred billion (100,000,000,000) of them. Even so, the newborn brain is still only a quarter of its adult size. As birth approaches, the brain cells start to grow long, branching extensions called dendrites, which form vast numbers of connections with other cells.

BUDDING BRAIN

The growth of dendrites and the formation of synapses (connections) continues at an astonishing pace through the first weeks and months of life, and it is this process of forming connections that is responsible for doubling the brain's size in the first year of life. Some connections become stronger through use. Eventually, they form networks that link different areas of the brain together, producing the mental abilities we rely on, such as speaking, and recognizing faces. Other, less useful connections will fade – a process called synaptic pruning, which frees up space to allow the more important connections to be strengthened.

Most of the brain's development after birth is in the cortex – the wrinkled top layer where all the "higher" mental functions (everything from vision to reasoning) are located. Underneath the cortex are other parts of the brain that support the essential functions of life, such as breathing and eating. While these "lower" areas drive much of a baby's behaviour in the early weeks of life, the immature cortex is also busy, processing the information from the baby's first experiences of the world.

FINAL DESTINATION

At birth, neurons (brain cells) have already travelled to their ultimate destination in the brain. This migration is completed during the last three months of pregnancy, and is largely determined by the genes. During migration, neurons climb along special fibres, which act as guides to make sure the neurons reach their correct destination.

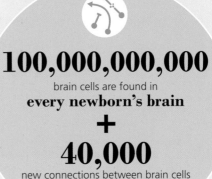

100,000,000,000

brain cells are found in
every newborn's brain

+

40,000

new connections between brain cells
are formed **every second**.

READY AND WAITING

Although it still has most of its growing to do, some parts of the cortex are waiting for particular experiences. When a newborn baby hears speech, brain activity increases on the left side, which is specialized for language. Similarly, hearing music activates the right side of the brain, and newborns listening to music show right-brain activity.

Somatosensory cortex This is the region of the brain that processes the sense of touch. Its early development explains why babies can recognize things through touch from birth, while recognition by sight comes later.

Auditory cortex In newborns, this area already responds to speech, especially on the left-hand side of the brain (where speech is processed in adults).

Frontal cortex
The command centre of the brain, which is very immature in newborns. Later on, it will be used to plan actions, control emotions and impulses, and provide the ability to focus on one task while ignoring distractions.

Visual cortex This area is where all the information coming in through the eyes is put together and processed. Although some areas of the visual cortex are functioning in newborns, this area is still very immature. A newborn baby is unable to control what she looks at, or to see anything in detail.

Olfactory cortex
This area, which sits behind and under the frontal cortex, is where smells are processed, so it is important in enabling the baby to find her mum's breast, and suckle.

Thalamus The area, which lies under the cortex, has many functions, most involving the senses. The thalamus receives information from the eyes, ears, and touch sensors, and sends it to the cortex for processing.

Amygdala This area in the central brain plays a key role in monitoring events that are crucial to survival. In adults, it tells us when there is something to be afraid of, but in newborn babies it is probably most useful in making them pay attention to all those faces in their environment that have so much to teach them.

Brain stem This is the key area for supporting life, enabling the baby to breathe, feel hungry, suck, and sleep.

REGION ACTIVITY

○ **Very active**

○ **Active**

○ **Less active**

Sleeping and dreaming

The need for sleep is greater in the first months of life than at any other time. Newborn babies can spend 18 hours a day sleeping, but what actually goes on in their heads when they sleep is far from clear.

THE FUNCTION OF SLEEP IS ONE of the great mysteries of human biology. Young babies spend two-thirds of the time asleep, and even adults spend a third of their lives asleep, yet exactly why we need to sleep so much isn't clear. It's not just a way of saving energy. Like all animals, we do more than just rest when we sleep – our brains block out the barrage of information from the senses and shut down conscious awareness. This suggests that sleep is vital to the way our brains develop and work.

LEARNING WHILE SLEEPING

A baby's brain grows faster than any other organ in the first months of life – but as well as growing it is absorbing information and learning. Studies suggest that sleep is vital to the process of learning: the amount of nighttime sleep a baby has at 12 months is correlated with her vocabulary at 26 months. Some scientists believe the brain uses sleep to strengthen or prune the connections between brain cells, thereby consolidating memories.

TYPICAL PATTERNS OF SLEEP IN BABIES, CHILDREN, AND ADULTS

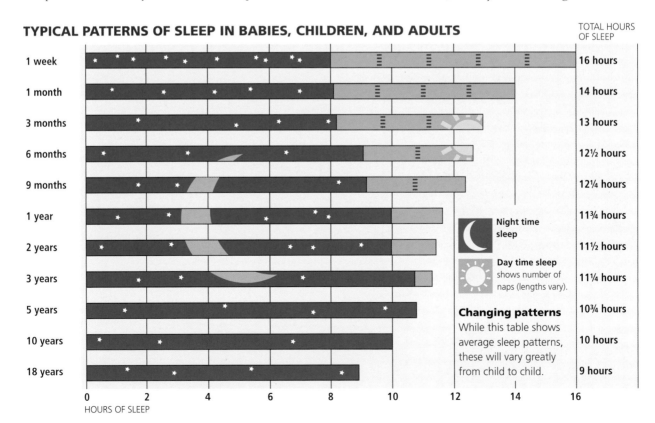

	TOTAL HOURS OF SLEEP
1 week	16 hours
1 month	14 hours
3 months	13 hours
6 months	12½ hours
9 months	12¼ hours
1 year	11¾ hours
2 years	11½ hours
3 years	11¼ hours
5 years	10¾ hours
10 years	10 hours
18 years	9 hours

Night time sleep

Day time sleep shows number of naps (lengths vary).

Changing patterns While this table shows average sleep patterns, these will vary greatly from child to child.

HOURS OF SLEEP

A NEWBORN SLEEP CYCLE
Unlike an adult's more complex sleep cycle,
a baby experiences just two stages of sleep.
First is "active" sleep, followed by the
deeper stage of "quiet" sleep.

Active sleep

STAGE1 Active sleep comes first and is
similar to adult rapid eye movement (REM)
sleep, which is when dreams occur.
Whether babies dream, too, is unknown.
Active sleep is characterized by
frequent jerky movements as
well as sounds.

Quiet sleep

STAGE 2 This second stage of the cycle
is when the baby sinks into a deeper level
of sleep. Quiet sleep is characterized by
the baby's body becoming far more still,
displaying very few movements, and
a calm, rhythmic breathing.

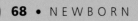

CHANGING CYCLE

A baby's sleeping pattern changes fast. Her eyes pick up the daily cycle of light and dark (day to night) which sets her internal biological clock, creating a preference for sleeping at night within a few months.

Newborn

She sleeps approximately **16–18 hours a day,** in about **seven short stints** throughout the **day and night.**

1 month

A baby will typically sleep for around **14 hours in a 24 hour period,** usually with **four naps** during the day.

2 years

A child sleeps **9–10 hours** at night, and typically naps **once** during the day, for **one to two hours** – usually at lunchtime. So the majority of his sleeping is at night.

1 year

A typical one-year-old sleeps around **12 hours** in total and will need to nap **one to two** times during the day. Usually, by this age a child is sleeping through the night.

3 months

Nightime sleep periods grow longer and **daytime naps** settle into a pattern. The ability to sleep **through the night** without regular feeding does not develop until a baby weighs about **6kg (13lb)**.

6 months

She now sleeps about **12–13 hours** in total. A typical baby naps **two to three** times during the day and sleeps about **nine hours** in total at night, with the longest continuous sleep episode lasting up to **six hours**.

CYCLICAL SLEEP

For the first nine months, babies sleep in cycles of 50–60 minutes. At the end of a cycle a baby will wake up, or may continue sleeping for a while.

WAKEY WAKEY

Babies are easily awakened in the first 25 minutes after falling asleep, making it hard to move a sleeping baby without waking her.

SLEEP CYCLES

Newborns spend a total of 16–18 hours asleep a day. They sleep in short bursts, seemingly at random, and spend as much time asleep in the day as at night. Sleep episodes vary in length but are usually under two hours, and a typical baby has about seven sleeps over the course of a day, separated by waking periods when she feeds. As she grows larger and needs to feed less frequently, her ability to sleep longer improves.

Measures of brain activity reveal that adults cycle through five stages of sleep. Most dreams occur in a stage called rapid eye movement (REM) sleep, when the eyes dart about under the lids. During REM sleep the brain is active, but motor signals to body muscles are blocked, preventing dreams from being acted out. Young babies have a simpler sleep cycle of only two stages: active and quiet. Active sleep is similar to adult REM sleep, but the blockade of motor signals is incomplete, so a baby may jerk, smile, grimace, or make sounds.

Active sleep is followed by a deeper stage called quiet sleep, when the baby stops moving, and her breathing becomes calm and rhythmic. She may make fast sucking motions during quiet sleep, and every now and then her body may "startle", but otherwise she remains still and is less easily roused than during active sleep.

SLEEP AND GROWTH

One reason babies need so much sleep may be that sleep is linked to growth. Growth hormone is secreted during sleep, and the body's metabolic processes tend to be anabolic (building up molecules, cells, and tissues) rather than catabolic (breaking them down). Studies of sleeping patterns in newborns reveal that extra naps sometimes lead to a small growth spurt.

DREAM TIME

Adults spend about 20 per cent of sleep time in REM sleep – the stage associated with dreaming. Newborns, however, spend half their sleep time in active sleep (equivalent to REM). But while measures of brain activity confirm that a baby's brain is working hard during active sleep, it isn't clear whether the baby is dreaming or not. Adults awoken during REM sleep in sleep laboratories nearly always report being in a dream, while three-year-olds report being in a dream less often – only 25 per cent of the time, according to one study. REM sleep in small children and active sleep in babies may, in fact, be mostly dreamless.

REM sleep may help to consolidate the type of memory needed to learn physical skills, such as walking, using the hands, or speaking. Another theory is that the waves of brain activity produced during REM sleep help the brain and nervous system develop by providing the additional stimulation needed for nerve cells to form circuits. If so, this might explain why babies spend so much of their time in active sleep.

The purpose of dreams, whether in children or adults, is a mystery. Some experts argue that dreams are meaningless stories created by the forebrain as it tries to make sense of random nerve signals generated without input from the senses. Other theories, linking sleep with learning, suggest dreams are rehearsals of daytime activities. Whatever the higher purpose of dreams may be, for now, at least, the mystery of dreaming will remain.

> *Sleep is vital to the process of learning… the amount of sleep a baby has at 12 months is correlated with her vocabulary at 26 months.*

Six stages of alertness

From the deepest sleep to vigorous crying, each different level of activity or rest is linked to how a newborn baby interacts with her world.

A warm bath, soft lights and music, and rocking can help prepare a baby for sleep.

DEEP SLEEP

Although the baby might jerk her body or make sucking movements with her mouth, she's sleeping soundly, and won't want to wake up to feed or play.

The baby is still and extremely relaxed; there's a slow rhythm to her breathing.

QUIET ALERT

The baby is at her most attentive, establishing eye contact and listening to people talking to her. She is calm and still, yet wide awake.

During this phase, the baby channels her energy into taking in the sights and sounds around her.

LIGHT SLEEP

The baby makes brief crying sounds, sucking motions, and displays a variety of facial expressions. She may cry quietly but doesn't need to be picked up.

The baby may respond to sounds, and move her arms and legs around.

DROWSY

In this state the baby is neither asleep nor awake; she may even startle from time to time. Her eyes may not focus, and her lids are droopy.

Although she is sleepy, the baby's activity level varies from active to inactive.

ACTIVE ALERT

The baby is either hungry or tired, and can't lie still. Although wide awake and restless, she is not as attentive as when in the quiet alert state.

In this state, the baby is unsettled; she puts her hand to her mouth, and may be hungry.

CRYING

The baby is agitated; her crying may signal that she is hungry or uncomfortable. Crying can be a release that enables her to move to another state of alertness.

The baby may move her arms and legs vigorously and contort her face. Soothing her makes her feel safe and secure again.

Feeling comfortable

A comfortable baby is a contented baby. As long as her mum is close at hand, and her physical and emotional needs are met, she will feel safe and secure.

FOR A NEWBORN BABY – who has been confined for nine months in a warm, dark womb – the reality of our big, bright world is quite a shock to the system. Suddenly she has to breathe for the first time, feel cold air on her skin instead of warm fluid, experience hunger, and process a whole array of sights, noises, and sensations. And the only way for her to register her displeasure is to cry. It is a whole new world, and the best way for a baby to be contented within it, is to feel comfortable.

PHYSICAL COMFORT

A baby's delicate skin is unused to exposure to air, so she is sensitive to physical sensations, such as temperature and touch. What's more, babies find it hard to regulate their body temperature, and they can become either cold or overheated easily. Newborn babies can't generate heat by shivering, instead they use a type of fat tissue called brown adipose to produce heat directly. They are

also born with a "startle" reflex – throwing the arms out to the side – which can be triggered in the womb by a sudden movement by their mother, as well as by drowsiness. For these reasons, new babies are often most comfortable in a warm, enclosed space with muted lighting and relative quiet, as it replicates the environment of the womb, helping them to feel safe.

EMOTIONAL COMFORT

A baby can't communicate her wants or needs, and can show distress only by crying. She has no sophisticated requirements, so her most important and immediate emotional need is to bond with her parents in order to feel secure. Close, physical contact with a parent – particularly the mother – is vital to a baby's sense of security: being able to feel her mother's heartbeat, hear her voice, and smell her familiar smell reduces a baby's stress levels and offers a profound source of comfort.

KANGAROO CARE

Babies take emotional comfort from "skin-to-skin" contact (kangaroo care), which also has many physiological benefits. It helps to establish body temperature, stabilize their heart and breathing rates, reduce the risk of severe illness and infection, and bond with mum.

ALL TOO MUCH

A contented baby needs regular sleep, and being "overtired" will stop this from happening. A baby is born with an immature nervous system, and is able to process only one or two things happening at once – so being surrounded by too many points of stimulation will result in an overtired baby.

MORE STIMULATION

Just as they can hate too much stimulation, if not enough is done to rouse a baby's interest, it can make her uncomfortable since she may feel she has been abandoned. Sometimes, a baby may have no immediate needs, such as being hungry, but just wants to be cuddled or played with.

> Babies are often most comfortable in a warm, enclosed space, with muted lighting and relative quiet, as it replicates the environment of the womb…

Crying is exhausting for a baby, and hard for a parent to listen to: but this key means of communication is vital for a baby's wellbeing.

Cry baby

From feeling ill to needing a cuddle, the cause of a baby's distress can be conveyed to an adult only through crying. Initially, it's an instinctive response, but later she learns to use crying for her own purposes.

FOR A BABY, crying performs a very important function: communication. Before she is able to use language, crying is the only way a baby has to alert her parents to a problem. This basic instinct ensures that newborns are fed, cared for, not ignored, and is what gives them the best chance of survival. However, babies have many different reasons for crying, and it is incumbent on a parent to decide what the cry means.

PARENTAL RESPONSE

Crying has a significant effect on parents – and especially on mums, who have a connection with their baby that goes beyond the emotional. Brain imaging studies have revealed that men's and women's brains react differently to a baby's cry, suggesting that women are more "hard wired" to respond. When a baby cries, her mother's brain is active in the areas that process reward and motivation, leading her to respond by going to her baby. In mums who breastfeed, a baby's cries of hunger also trigger the release of the hormone oxytocin, which stimulates the breasts to produce milk in preparation for a feed. These physiological responses take place within about seven minutes of the cries starting.

WHAT'S UP?

Babies cry for many reasons, most of which are to do with them feeling some kind of discomfort: they may be too hot or too cold, they may be tired, hungry, have a soiled nappy, be ill, or in pain. They may even just fancy a cuddle with mum – and considering how long they have been held close in the womb, this isn't really surprising. Unfortunately for parents, there is no shortcut to understanding what the problem is!

COLICKY BABIES

The word "colic" strikes fear into a parent's heart, as it is synonymous with relentless, long-term crying. However, colic is a condition about which surprisingly little is known – even though some 20 per cent of babies may be affected by colic, starting a few weeks after birth and continuing during the first three to four months.

While the term was used in the past to mean painful, trapped wind, doctors now suspect that the physical signs we loosely term colic – crying frequently, making fists of the hands, pulling the legs up towards the abdomen, and seeming to have pains in the stomach – may be due to other factors. Colic is now used mainly as

Studies have revealed that men's and women's brains react differently to a baby's cry… women are more "hard-wired" to respond.

a term for excessive crying: if a baby cries for more than three hours at a time, for more than three days a week, and for over three weeks, she is considered to have colic. However, although distressing for both baby and parent, colic has no long-term ill effects on a baby's development and lasts for only a short time – though it may seem an eternity for the parents.

TYPES OF CRYING

Many people believe that babies use crying as a sort of language, indicating what they need by different types of cry. Current research suggests this isn't really true: the main difference is actually just volume. So, instead of a baby having distinct cries for hunger, pain, frustration, fear, feeling cold or tired, and so on, a baby will actually just cry more loudly the more discomfort she is in – and her parents will probably guess the reason.

One type of cry, however, is distinctive: the birth cry, which is quieter than the cries babies make later on. The birth cry perhaps evolved like this to avoid alerting predators to the vulnerable newborn and mum.

FAKING IT

As babies become more interested in the world around them, they begin to use crying to get results: not just when they are distressed, but because they want attention. And perhaps this is no bad thing: causing a reaction and being comforted is incredibly soothing for the baby, and

> Crying is exhausting, using 13% of a newborn's energy. Babies cry most at six weeks old.

CRYING THROUGH THE FIRST YEAR

0–2 MONTHS
Crying is a reflex in response to internal causes, such as hunger, tiredness, or discomfort. Until the source of crying is found, it is likely to continue.

2 MONTHS ONWARDS
Babies begin to cry in response to what's happening around them, or they may feel lonely. Crying attracts and directs a parent's attention to the baby's needs.

Feed me! I'm hungry!

I'm here! Cuddle me!

it can have a positive effect on the relationship between a baby and her parents. If a baby cries without tears and very soon smiles when the parent returns, it could be labelled as "fake crying", and may be frustrating for parents. But for the baby, the motivation seems to be born of a genuine love of interacting with her parents.

> *It opens the lungs, washes the countenance, exercises the eyes, and softens down the temper… so cry away.*

Charles Dickens (1812–1870)

HOLD ME CLOSE

In some cultures, babies cry very little and rarely suffer colic. The !Kung San tribe that lives on the plains of the Kalahari in Africa hold their babies constantly and breastfeed several times an hour – and colic is virtually unknown. Other cultures where the baby is held almost constantly – in a sling or papoose, for example – also experience shorter periods of crying and fewer incidences of colic. The babies' closeness with their parents, and a more upright position, may be among the reasons for this.

7–9 MONTHS ONWARDS

Crying begins to be a deliberate response – in fact, a baby is more likely to cry when her carer is nearby, hoping to prompt a reaction.

12 MONTHS ONWARDS

Babies can now "decide" when to cry or not, depending on their audience – so crying no longer reliably indicates an urgent, physical need.

Looking after baby

Parenting techniques – including how a child is cared for, as well as how she eats, sleeps, and potty-trains – have changed and evolved over time. And they all are remarkably different around the world.

CULTURES VARY WILDLY across the world, and nowhere is this more apparent than in attitudes towards parenting. From who takes on the role of primary carer to how a baby is put down for a nap, the decisions and traditions of child-rearing have evolved over the centuries, and continue to do so as cultures themselves change in accordance with the times.

THE PRIMARY CARER

In most societies around the world, it is the mother who has traditionally taken on the role of the baby's primary caregiver, usually assisted by other female members of the family, such as sisters, aunts, and grandmothers. In contemporary Western society, a baby's mother still tends to be the primary caregiver, although some fathers are now starting to take on a more central role. As traditional gender roles change and develop, it's becoming increasingly common for fathers to take paternity leave, and some couples decide that the father should stay at home after the baby's birth rather than the mother, especially if the mother is the higher earner.

In Scandinavian countries, such as Sweden, the emphasis is less on the mother than on the family unit as a whole. Though the mother's role as primary caregiver is not challenged, particularly if she is breastfeeding, the concept of gender equality is a fundamental part of most Nordic countries' laws and culture. A Swedish family is offered 16 months parental leave, and the couple can choose how they split that between them, with the exception of two months' leave that can be taken only by the mum. So a baby is used to having both parents around, which can help to strengthen family bonds.

THE "GRANDMOTHER HYPOTHESIS"

Throughout many cultures, the grandmother is an important caregiver, helping with the day-to-day care of her grandchild so that the parents can continue to work.

As well as being a great help to women wishing to resume their career after having a baby, the huge amount of help that grandmothers provide may also explain something of an evolutionary enigma: why human females live decades beyond their reproductive years, while our closest relatives – the chimpanzees – tend to die soon after their fertile years are over. Known as the "grandmother hypothesis", this theory suggests that grandmothers have the resources and energy to care for children even though their own reproductive days are past. A grandmother can then help support her daughters and daughters-in-law, allowing them to have

THE GRANDMOTHER EFFECT

A study that looked at women in Finland during the 1700s and 1800s, found that the longer a woman lived beyond her childbearing years, the more grandchildren were born in her family: two extra grandchildren were born for every 10 years that she lived beyond the menopause.

more babies at shorter intervals and giving those babies a better chance of survival. She will also pass on more copies of her own longevity genes through her children and their offspring.

A study that helped form this theory saw grandmothers in Tanzania's Hadza tribe gathering food for their grandchildren. Non-human mammals collect their own food after weaning, but if grandmothers help children too young to gather their own food, this not only supports the survival of the young, but also helps the group as a whole to function and reproduce frequently.

Sharing the load The sharing of parental duties is normal in Scandinavian countries. This helps create a strong family bond as the baby becomes accustomed to the constant presence of both parents.

> *Throughout many cultures, the grandmother is an important caregiver, helping with the day-to-day care of her grandchild.*

SLEEPY TIME

Attitudes concerning how much, where, and when a baby sleeps vary around the world. In northern Europe, parents often put babies to sleep in their own room, by six or seven o'clock. However, in southern European countries – Spain, for example – parents include the infant at the family dinner, allowing them to play, chat, or sleep, before putting them to bed later on.

In the past, particularly in communities where dwellings were quite primitive, babies would have slept when they needed to, and where they slept would not have been so important. In some rural communities today this is still the case: in Kenya's Luhya tribe, where most people work on the land, a baby is kept with her mother almost all day in a sling on her back. At night, the baby sleeps on the floor of a hut with the mother nearby, so the idea of bedtime for the baby is unknown.

SUN AND AIR

During the 1920s, the child welfare reformer Frederic Truby King advised that babies should be put outside to sleep, so that they could get as much sun as possible. Families without gardens could purchase a metal cage that hung from the window! Parents are now more afraid of skin cancer, and skin protection for children in the sun has become a priority. However, in the last few years, children in countries with short days during the winter, such as the UK and Scandinavia, are prone to vitamin D deficiency. In the UK, the incidence of rickets increased four-fold in the first 14 years of the 21st century. As a result, children are recommended to take dietary supplements, and to spend time in the sun – as long as they are properly protected with a high-factor sun cream.

In Scandinavia, babies are put outside to nap, even in winter. The belief is that napping in the fresh air can help prevent diseases. A study of children's health has shown limited evidence that the incidence of coughs and colds is lower in cultures where babies nap indoors. But since the children are well wrapped up, their clothing restricts movement, which may help them to nap longer than they would indoors.

POTTIES, NAPPIES, AND DOING WITHOUT

Nappy-wearing ideas differ around the world and have changed over time. In the developed world, babies potty-train later than they used to, mostly due to the fact that disposable nappies mean they never feel wet, and thus get a mental cue for starting to potty-train. It's also easier for parents to carry on with nappies since they don't have the chore of washing and drying cloth nappies, which led mums in the past to want to potty-train as early as possible.

Disposable nappies were first produced in the 1930s and, of course, are the norm today. But due to the environmental impact of nappies being thrown into landfill, and the resources and energy used to produce them, cloth nappies are now making something of a comeback.

In some cultures, where mothers carry their babies almost constantly while working in the fields, the mums can become so attuned to their babies that they can anticipate toilet needs, listening out for little clues and cries. They then hold the baby over the soil to relieve herself, without having many "accidents" or needing much in the way of nappies. This method, called "elimination communication", has been adopted – with varying amounts of success – by some Western families.

LYING IN

In Japan, mothers traditionally rested in their own home for 100 days after a birth, although modern Japanese women are no longer expected to do so. However, they do tend to stay in hospital longer than Western women – at least four to seven days. Interestingly, the lower incidence of uterine disease and hysterectomies in later life in Japanese women may be as a result of this resting period.

ROUTINES AROUND THE WORLD

The many parenting techniques for putting babies to sleep – from strapping them to a mother's back to quietly laying them in a darkened room – have evolved differently around the world to suit the needs of different cultures.

Sleeping on the go While in Western societies, concerns over whether to use a cot or Moses baskets can take a fair amount of consideration, in some communities babies go to work with their parents and sleep as they need to, while strapped on their mother's back.

{ Various materials were once used for nappies, such as milkweed, moss, and linen. }

Staying up late South Asians tend to dine relatively late, and part of their culture is to include a baby or child in the dining experience, so they can all interact socially as a family.

Keep it dark In Western countries, parents prefer to keep their baby in a darkened room during nap times.

In the fresh air Encouraging babies to spend time outdoors – whatever the season – is a Scandinavian tradition. The short days in Scandinavian countries mean time outside is important for children to ensure they get sufficient vitamin D.

{ It's likely that very young babies' emotions are far simpler than those of older babies. }

Developing emotion Early newborn responses (right) give way to more defined expressions by six weeks (opposite). From around three months, more complex emotions will show.

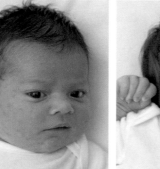

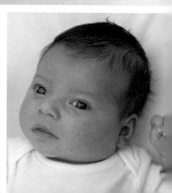

First feelings

Even very small babies appear to show their feelings – through crying or looks of contentment – but even with scientific methods it's a puzzle to work out exactly what they are feeling.

NO ONE CAN REMEMBER what it feels like to be born, but it must be distressing to be expelled from a warm, snug womb into the bright, cold world outside. It's not surprising that a baby's first response is to cry. But what do a baby's cries indicate – just discomfort, or are they real emotions, such as anger or fear?

INSTINCTIVE RESPONSE

It is likely that very young babies' emotions are far simpler than those of older babies and adults. A "happy" newborn is probably just feeling safe and comfortable; and if not, she will feel and show distress. As a baby grows out of the newborn phase, she will be able to experience more complex emotions.

EMOTIONAL RESPONSE

By about three months old, a baby can be seen to experience at least five adult emotions: joy, interest, anger, sadness, and disgust. Although we can't tell directly what babies experience, it is possible to get some idea of what's going on in their brains by using a brain imaging technique called functional magnetic resonance imaging (fMRI).

From the age of three months, babies' brains seem to respond to certain emotions in a similar way to adults: in one study, when infants heard sad and fearful voices, the region of the brain that's involved in dealing with these emotions in adults also became active in the babies.

Babies' feelings can also be assessed in terms of how they react to emotion in others. Researchers have found that 10-week-old babies show anger, cry, or just freeze when their mothers look and sound angry, turn away if she looks sad, and smile when she seems happy. This, the researchers argue, suggests that seeing emotions in others makes even young babies respond with matching emotions of their own.

> Even when they are just A FEW DAYS OLD, babies will cry in EMPATHY when they hear ANOTHER BABY CRY.

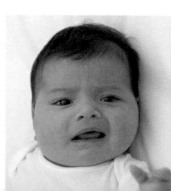

Senses

New world of the senses

When babies are born, they begin to share our sensory world – but they experience that world in a very different way.

IF WE COULD GO BACK IN TIME and re-experience our first few days, it might feel as strange as a hallucinogenic trip. As adults, we take it for granted that we see sights, hear sounds, and smell odours. Yet a newborn baby has no concept of these distinct sensory experiences. And although newborns are more aware of the environment around them than was once believed, research suggests that a baby's senses may still be strongly intermingled – perhaps resembling the "blooming, buzzing confusion" that philosopher William James speculated over 100 years ago.

WHICH SENSE IS WHICH?

In fact, newborn babies may not be able to distinguish one sense from another at all. This may seem improbable, but some adults experience a similar condition, called synaesthesia, which is when a sensation in one sense produces a perception in another. It is widely believed that for the Russian painter Wassily Kandinsky, different colours were associated with particular sounds, such as those of orchestral instruments. And as a child, he reportedly "heard" his paintbox hiss when he mixed the colours. In 2011, a study showed that three-month-old babies do have synaesthesia-like associations between shapes and colours, which were not found in eight-month-olds.

> If we could go back in time and re-experience our first few days, it might feel as strange as a hallucinogenic trip.

The cause of synaesthesia seems to be a crossover of connections in the brain between different senses. At birth, this is the norm: the brain's neural connections are not yet honed by experience into specific sensory pathways. In time, cross-connections between the senses have usually been pruned away or no longer work, producing the separate senses that become familiar.

The human ability to make sense of cross-sensory metaphors, such as a "sharp taste" or a "loud pattern", may even be a leftover from the early sensory interminglings of our infancy.

MAKING SENSE OF IT

If the idea of being unaware of different senses seems weird, an analogy is the way that we view three-dimensional objects. The human brain unconsciously combines separate elements of visual perceptions, such as perspective, light and shade, and the slightly shifted viewpoints from both eyes – into a three-dimensional image, without us being aware of the varied sources of information.

Similarly, although a newborn baby's brain may not be able to work out which sense the information is coming from, it might still all add up to a comprehensible experience for the baby.

> The baby, assailed by eyes, ears, nose, skin… feels it all as one great blooming, buzzing confusion.

William James, US philosopher and psychologist (1842–1910)

Developing senses

At birth, some of a baby's senses are at a different stage of development than others, so it's a game of catch-up for some senses during the first few months.

 SIGHT

This sense gets going only at birth, but develops to become the most important. Newborns are unable to see fine details – these need to be 30 times bolder than for adults – so a lot of patterns and textures look plain. In the early weeks, babies prefer contrasting patterns, like chequerboards.

 TASTE

Newborn babies may not have much of a sense of taste, but at two weeks old they have already learned to like sweet flavours and dislike bitter ones. The naturally sweet taste of breast milk suits a baby perfectly.

 SMELL

The senses of smell and taste are closely linked, and a newborn will show preference for a sweet scent, such as milk, and show aversion to an unpleasant or pungent smell.

 HEARING

When a baby is born, her sense of hearing is well developed. Newborns can hear a similar range of sounds to adults – including low-pitched sounds – but they prefer sounds at speaking pitch.

 TOUCH

For newborns, touch is hugely important as it lowers stress hormones and makes the baby feel calm. Other associated stimuli, such as temperature, also can have a strong effect – warmth is comforting, and seems to block pain and reduce crying. Gently massaging a baby's highly sensitive skin can be extremely soothing, and research has found that it helps to reduce crying.

 MOVEMENT

Babies receive sensory information from ligaments and joints, and from tiny sense organs within their muscles. This tells the brain what each part of the body is doing, and provides the foundation for learning body awareness and movement. Initially babies make jerky reflex movements.

 BALANCE

Gravity receptors in the inner ear, eyes, and muscles provide sensory information related to movement and balance. These senses allow a baby to maintain balance while still or moving. One study shows that babies who were taken swimming from an early age had better balance and grasping skills.

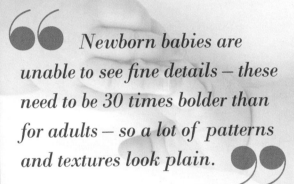

Newborn babies are unable to see fine details — these need to be 30 times bolder than for adults — so a lot of patterns and textures look plain.

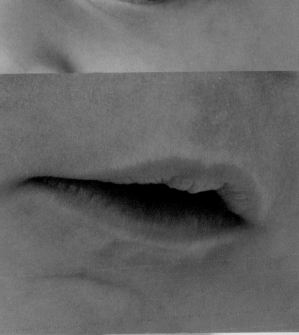

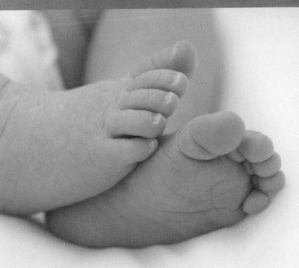

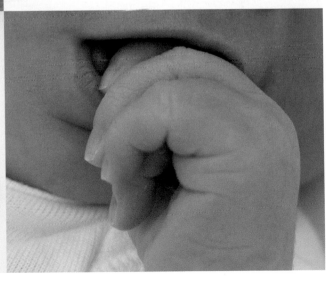

Learning to see

Between birth and 12 months, a baby's blurry,
formless, monochrome world becomes a riot of colour
and shade, detail and depth.

BIRTH–2 MONTHS

A two-week-old baby gazes up at her mother and knows her by sight alone. But she isn't detecting the shape of her mother's nose, or the colour of her eyes. Research suggests it's the basic outline of a face and the hairline that a young baby relies upon for recognition. At this point, her ciliary muscles (which change the shape of the lens) and her extraocular muscles (which move her eyes) are still weak. This means she has trouble focusing an image on her retina. At this age, she understands shapes by spotting contrast, and she finds large black-and-white patterns most appealing. She also likes to watch things that are moving – like her mother's lips, falling leaves, or a brightly coloured mobile turning against a pale wall. By two months, as well as seeing contrasts in brightness, such as black and white and shades of grey, she can also distinguish red and green. However, she is unable to tell the difference between two similar hues, such as emerald and turquoise.

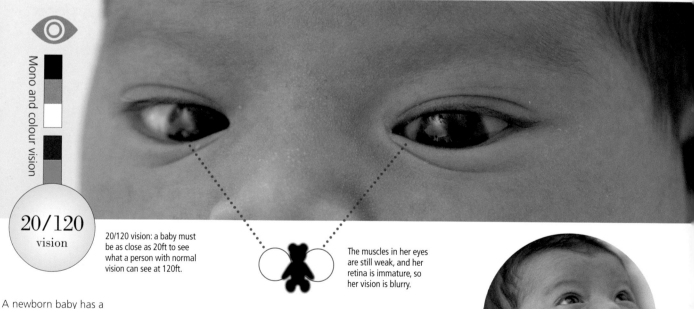

Mono and colour vision

20/120
vision

20/120 vision: a baby must be as close as 20ft to see what a person with normal vision can see at 120ft.

A newborn baby has a visual acuity of 20/120. If the baby could read, she would be able to read only the big "E" at the top of an eye chart.

The muscles in her eyes are still weak, and her retina is immature, so her vision is blurry.

At 0–2 months, she sees the world by spotting contrast, and she finds large black-and-white, high-contrast patterns most appealing; colour vision is limited at this stage. She can focus on objects that are about 20–38cm (8–15in) away.

BABY SEES...

A newborn baby can't see well at first. Her retina is still developing, so she won't be able to see details or colours. By around four months of age, everything becomes much clearer as the baby's visual system matures through experience.

1 WEEK 1
Mum's face is a simple outline shape.

2 MONTH 1
No colour but more detail.

3 MONTH 2
Some colour vision.

4 MONTH 4
Better detail, good colour.

2–4 MONTHS

A baby spots something interesting and fixes on it, then flicks to another object with confidence. At about three months, a baby's extraocular muscles are strong enough (and the connections between her eyes and her brain have developed sufficiently) that she can begin to track moving objects with her eyes. At first, though, these movements are jerky. Although she can now control her eyes well and focus a clear image, the fovea – the region of the retina that detects detail (as well as colour) – is still developing.

The parts of her brain responsible for processing visual signals, and making them meaningful, are also immature, so the world is still blurry. By four months, a baby has about 20/60 vision. This means that, when she is positioned 6m (20ft) from a object, she can see only as much detail that someone with normal 20/20 vision could see at 18m (60ft). However, the world is brighter; she can now see blue and yellow, and spot the difference between more subtle shades than she could a few months before.

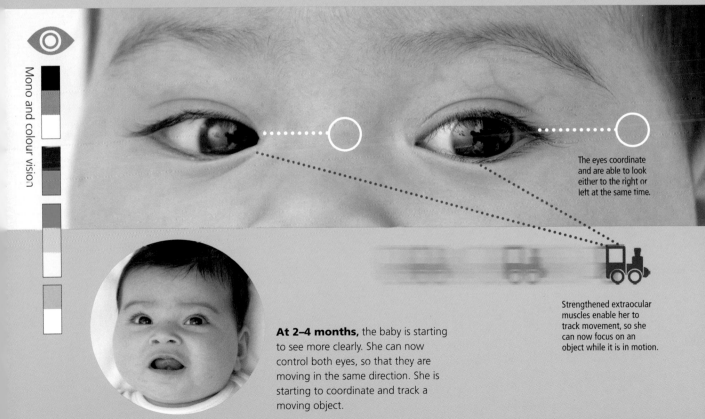

Mono and colour vision

The eyes coordinate and are able to look either to the right or left at the same time.

Strengthened extraocular muscles enable her to track movement, so she can now focus on an object while it is in motion.

At 2–4 months, the baby is starting to see more clearly. She can now control both eyes, so that they are moving in the same direction. She is starting to coordinate and track a moving object.

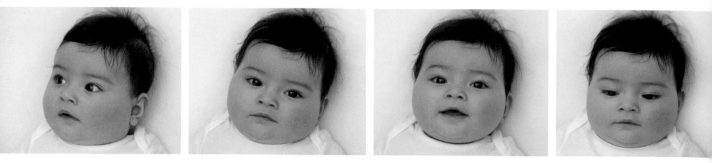

4–6 MONTHS

A six-month-old baby can gaze up at her father and take in the hairs in his eyebrows and the creases around his smiling eyes. She can also easily tell the difference between his face and that of a nearly identical uncle. Her colour vision is now well developed – if her bedroom is painted in various pastel shades, she should now be able easily to appreciate that they are different. By this age, she should be able to smoothly follow a moving object (in contrast to the jerky tracking eye movements of

earlier months). But there are still crucial disparities between the way a six-month-old sees the world and the way an adult would see it. She is starting to perceive depth, and has much better control of her arms. She may be eager to try to reach out to a toy or a hand to grab it – but she isn't always successful. However, she may manage to grab someone's hair or face, or even a fancy earring! Her vision is good enough to recognize people and objects across the other side of a room.

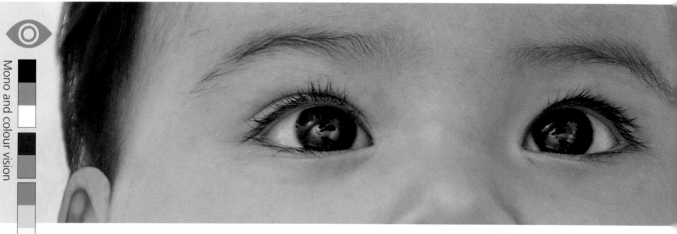

Mono and colour vision

Between four and six months of age, everything is becoming clearer. She is beginning to appreciate many different colours.

20/60 vision

With acuity of 20/60, a baby sees at 20ft what someone with normal vision can see clearly at 60ft.

Depth perception

By the age of four to six months, as well as smoothly tracking a moving object, she is starting to perceive depth. When she sees an interesting toy, she will try to get hold of it, but won't always be able to manage it.

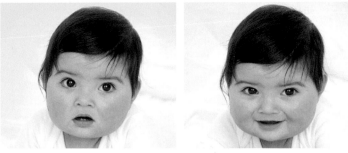

6–8 MONTHS

The baby rocks on her hands and her knees, and takes her first shuffling movements forwards. Learning to crawl not only helps her to reach interesting-looking objects, it helps her develop coordination between her eyes, hands, and feet. She also finds it easier to look for things, moving her eyes more and her head much less. While she still likes gazing at the faces of family and friends, she may also enjoy concentrating on other familiar images – such as pictures in a book.

8 MONTHS PLUS

With 20/30 vision, an eight-month-old baby can see detail almost as well as an adult. The muscles in her eyes are also so strong that she can easily focus on people on the other side of a room. Developments in her brain are also influencing what she uses her eyes for. If she drops a toy, she'll look for it. And her colour perception has also improved hugely: a seven- to eight-month-old baby can tell the difference between more subtle shades than just a few months earlier – like between gold and yellow.

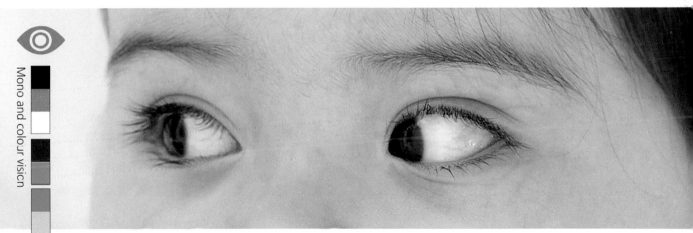

Mono and colour vision

By eight months, the baby will be able to see detail very well, and distinguish between shades of a colour.

20/30 vision

With a ratio of 20/30, a baby can see to a distance of 20ft; someone with normal acuity would see sharply to a distance of 30ft.

Colour vision develops At around six months, a baby's eye for detail will be getting better, and colour vision is also well advanced. She can already distinguish between similar strong colours. More subtle pastel shades can also be differentiated easily.

Crawling towards an object At six to eight months, a baby will deliberately crawl to reach something of interest. At the same time this activity is improving coordination between her hands, feet, and eyes, which are now moving more without her having to turn her head.

Getting focused

Babies love to gaze at things – and this activity is essential in the first six months to develop connections between the eyes and the brain. Even at a young age, they know what they like to look at.

WHEN A BABY IS BORN, her visual system is still under construction. As she starts exploring her own, close-up world with her eyes, this experience stimulates development in the brain areas that deal with vision. Research into babies who are temporarily unable to see during the first weeks, shows that many do not develop as accurate eyesight as babies born with normal sight. This is attributed to them missing out on the massive increase in connections that takes place in the visual cortex of the brain in response to early visual stimulation.

By the age of two months, a baby's muscles have developed to the extent that they can coordinate eye movements and focus the eyes together. This allows the brain to acquire visual information about an object, such as a toy, from two different angles, helping the baby to work out how far away her toy really is (depth perception). Accurate depth perception takes time to acquire, but it's one of the most vital visual skills. It allows her to grab a proffered snack, or to stop in her tracks if she is crawling and suddenly finds herself at the top of a flight of steps.

All babies find faces fascinating. Scientists now think that babies are born with a "face detector", which makes sure the baby sees lots of faces as her brain develops, so she can become a face expert. Babies aged one to three months spend about a quarter of their waking lives looking at faces.

HOW FAR, HOW DEEP?

If a two-month-old takes a swipe at a mobile, the odds are she'll miss. It's not until the age of three to four months that a baby starts to develop a sense of distance and depth.

In the first few weeks of life, babies prefer to look at **"face-like"** pictures, even if these are not at all lifelike: an image with just three black dots placed in the usual configuration of **two eyes** and **a mouth** will grab their attention.

Newborns see the world in black and white. At first they see patterns with **100%** contrast best, but by nine weeks they can distinguish between **two shades of grey** that differ by only 0.5% in brightness. This is not far off the **adult** sensitivity of **0.2%.**

Colour and pattern

As the inner structures of a baby's eye develop, she will learn
to distinguish between different colours and patterns – initially,
bright and bold is the name of the game.

BOLD OR BLACK AND WHITE

At birth, a baby's retina – the part of the
eye responsible for perception of colour
– isn't fully developed, so newborns
prefer looking at large, black and white
patterns, such as spots and stripes.
They are also drawn to bold, contrasting
colours, since these help them to
distinguish shapes.

BABIES' FAVOURITE COLOURS

Babies as young as four months have favourite colours,
according to research by the University of Surrey, UK.
Researchers studied babies aged between four and nine
months, and found that some showed a striking preference for
just one colour, while others favoured a few. Children from
different cultures have the same reaction to colours, suggesting
that preferences are initially not dependent on experience.

Colour blindness is
caused by problems with
the cells in the eye that see
colour. It's often undetected
until a child is a few
years old.

**Colours can affect
mood:** babies shown
shades of blue became
bored, but brightened up
when presented with
a change of colour.

**Babies appear
to prefer** richer shades
of blue, bright orange,
purple, and red, and
looked longer at these
than at brown.

Babies may not
be able to tell the
difference between
subtle pastel colours
until they are about
six months old.

When learning
the names of the
colours, toddlers usually
named brown and grey
last of all – these were
the colours they
liked least.

" ... *Babies as young as four months have favourite colours... Some showed a striking preference for just one colour, while others favoured a few.* "

Babies group colours into categories, such as blue, green, yellow, and red, even before they acquire language. These categories are found across different cultures.

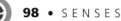

Illusion confusion

The world is a bewildering place for babies, especially when their developing visual systems play tricks on them. What's real and what's not? Is it really small or is it just far away?

I can't get hold of it!
At less than one year old, a baby doesn't understand that two-dimensional shapes are not real objects. The baby will probably try to pick the shape off the page – and may be confused when she can't.

That's better
Given the choice between a toy and a picture, a baby will probably go for the more explorer-friendly toy.

Two-dimensional
The baby isn't so interested in the picture when there is a real truck to play with.

Three-dimensional
There's no confusion about the allure of this toy tipper truck.

SIZING IT UP

A three-month-old lying in her cot gazes at a "small" teddy on her shelf. When her mother later bends over the cot and produces the same teddy from behind her back, the baby smiles at this new "big" bear. Learning that objects actually stay the same size is a crucial development, not least because this allows her to estimate distance. This concept, called size constancy, seems to begin to develop at about four months, then improves slowly. At about six to eight months, a baby understands that the teddy is the same one whether it's close to her face or 70cm (28in) away – but at this age, she has trouble when an object is more than 1m (39in) away from her. A full appreciation of size constancy takes years to acquire.

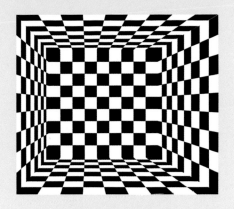

3 metres

2 metres

1 metre

The three bears
She knows it's the same bear, but it seems to come in three sizes!

GETTING IT INTO PERSPECTIVE

A two-dimensional pattern can trick the brain into thinking it is three-dimensional. By the time a baby is five to seven months old, she begins to fall for the illusion of perspective created by a chequerboard pattern where the lines look as if they are receding. Illusions reveal the mental leaps our brains make in interpreting visual data. Usually, these leaps help to make sense of the world – but they can deceive us. Here, the flat pattern looks like a five-sided box.

IS IT REAL?

Young babies who spot a favourite character in a book or on TV may reach out and try to grab it. This is because until she is about a year old, a baby has trouble understanding that 2D images are representations of an object, and not the real thing.

Typical nine-month-olds will often treat objects pictured in baby books as if they are the real thing, for example by trying to pluck them off the page, or even hitting out at them. But it isn't just babies who grow up in Western cultures who react like this: in countries where babies see far fewer pictures they respond in the same way. The more realistic the picture is, such as a colour photograph rather than a black-and-white drawing, the more likely it is that a baby under a year old will treat it as real. Although, equally, if a baby is offered a choice between having a real toy and a picture of one, they'll go for the real thing.

PUTTING A NAME TO IT

By the time a baby is 18 months old, she will usually have reached the stage where she will point to a picture, or try to name it. She's now learned that a picture is a representation, and this crucial mental development means she is starting to understand the use of symbols – which is the basis of language.

Sounds good

A baby's hearing starts to work well before birth. However, her ability to detect different sounds, and to make sense of them, develops dramatically during the first year of life.

BIRTH TO 2 MONTHS

The cells in a baby's cochlea – her inner ear – continue to mature after birth. So, too, does the auditory nerve, which carries sound information from the ear to the brain. A one-month-old will turn her head in the direction of a loud noise (though this ability dips at two months), and she becomes gradually better at detecting quieter noises.

2–4 MONTHS

The part of the brain that processes signals from the ears – the auditory cortex – is still developing. An adult-like brain response to sounds of different pitch is in place by about three months, though this response improves with age. A baby still prefers higher-pitched voices, and particularly her mother's voice when she engages in "baby talk". Babies also like to hear singing.

A baby still prefers higher-pitched voices, and particularly her mother's voice when she engages in "baby talk". She also likes to hear singing.

Workings of the ear

Sound waves enter the ear and are funnelled into the ear canal, where they make the eardrum vibrate. The small bones of the middle ear amplify these vibrations and transmit them to the cochlea. Here, sensory cells convert the vibrations into nerve impulses, which travel to the brain where they are interpreted.

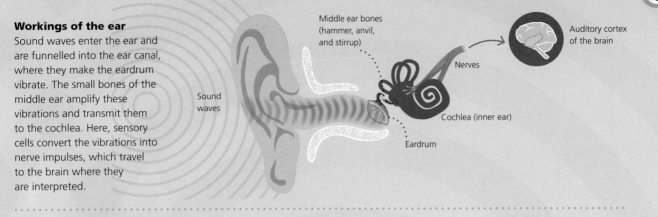

Middle ear bones (hammer, anvil, and stirrup)

Auditory cortex of the brain

Nerves

Sound waves

Cochlea (inner ear)

Eardrum

4–6 MONTHS

A baby's enjoyment of music – and sensitivity to rhythm – enters a new phase when she can coordinate her own movements in response to hearing a tune. A study of babies aged five months and over found that the better they could synchronize the waving of their arms and legs to a beat (as judged by professional ballet dancers), the more they smiled.

6 MONTHS PLUS

By about seven months, a baby can distinguish different timbres – as with the same note played by a violin and a guitar. But her perception of complex sounds, such as speech, is still immature, and even at twelve months she can't detect individual words against background noise as well as adults can. The auditory cortex continues to develop until late in adolescence.

Loud sounds: Surprisingly, a baby's cry close up can measure 115 decibels; that's nearly as loud as attending a rock concert, at 115–120 decibels!

Touch and learn

The first sense to develop – touch – is vital for a baby.
It can be a very effective source of reassurance, and plays
a key role in helping a baby learn to communicate.

A YOUNG BABY HELD CLOSE in her mother's arms feels secure and safe, and this is largely due to sensory stimulation of the largest organ in her body – her skin. Even a newborn baby is used to the comfort provided by gentle touch – this sense develops as early as the eighth week in the uterus, and by the fifth month, a fetus will touch her own face, and even put her thumb or fingers in her mouth.

Although the skin contains receptors specifically adapted to detect pressure, other types of receptor play a crucial role in what we think of as "touch", including those that detect stretching, pain, and temperature. Together these receptors make up the somatosensory system. While this is well developed even before a baby is born, it improves with experience. As a baby is stroked, cuddled, and dressed, she begins to know whether she's being brushed by a smooth and firm hand, or the fur of a soft toy.

MASSAGE
Infant massage is common in some cultures. It's widely used in South Asia, and Indian Ayurvedic medicine advocates a daily massage from birth. Recent research has found that massage – with long, reasonably firm strokes across the body – can reduce crying and improve sleeping, and may help premature babies to put on weight.

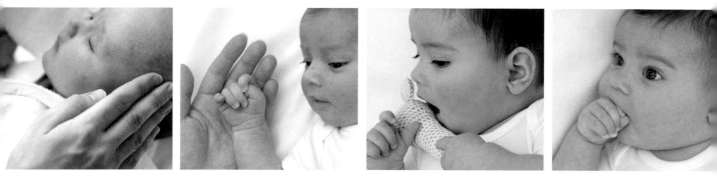

BIRTH TO 1 MONTH
Young babies know when they're being touched, and one study found that even sleeping babies of this age can detect touch. Babies who were stroked on one spot, such as the lips, stirred if the stroking moved to another part of their body, such as the ear.

1–6 MONTHS
The lips and tongue are rich in touch receptors. Once a baby can grasp an object, she'll put it in her mouth, and also start to suck her fingers. Between four and six months, she starts to distinguish between coarse textures, and will enjoy touchy-feely toys and books.

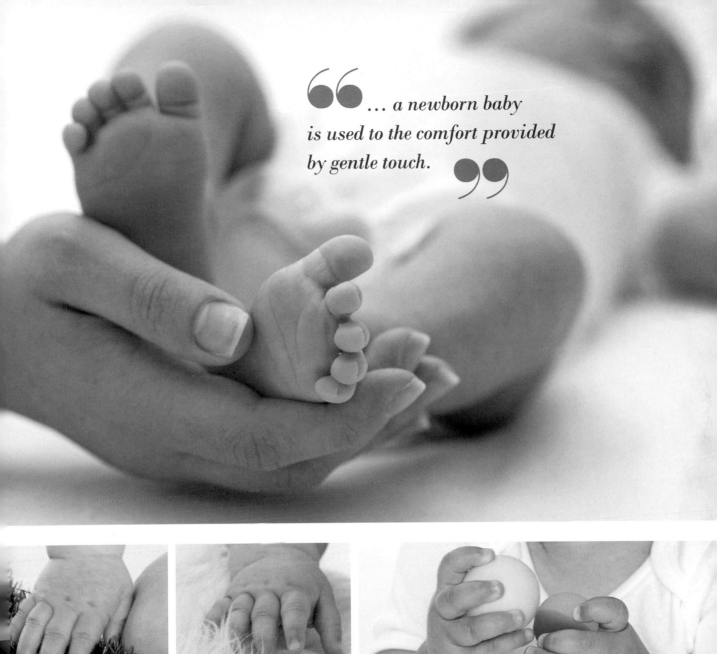

> *... a newborn baby is used to the comfort provided by gentle touch.*

6–12 MONTHS

By this age, a baby's ability to use touch, and explore different textures to learn about her world, is gradually improving. But there's still a way to go before it's fully mature. At one year of age, she can't use touch alone to distinguish different sizes and shapes: for example, given two balls that she can feel but can't see, she can't work out which is bigger. In fact, that skill will take a year or two to develop. And her tactile acuity – her ability to detect fine detail using her fingertips – won't peak until she's between 10 and 16 years of age.

Learning about balance
Finding her feet

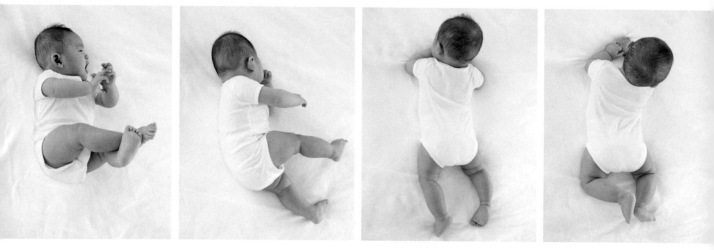

Learning to roll over into a position that allows the baby to push up, is the first stage in starting to crawl. Technique is everything!

The art of sitting upright initially requires a hand or two for balance. This builds up vital muscle strength in the arms.

Start with a balanced sitting position, then lean forward onto the hands. On your marks, get set, and go!

Once a baby manages to combine balance, muscle control, and strength, there is no holding her back – after a few initial wobbles, she's up and running!

Balancing on one leg When a baby first stands up and starts cruising around the furniture, her balance is rather unsteady. Her feet are not flat on the floor, since she hasn't learned to stretch out her toes. As her feet lengthen, the toes splay out, helping to keep her upright.

Getting around The baby's legs are widely spaced as the hip joints are still in an outward-leaning "frog" position. They gradually turn inwards as the baby learns to stand upright. Push-along toys help give stability.

BETTER BALANCE
There is evidence to show that babies who are taught to swim at a very young age develop a better sense of balance, earlier than their peers. Scientists at the Norwegian University of Science and Technology followed babies for five years and saw a marked increase in balance ability in babies who swam from the age of two months.

A sense of taste

Babies are born with fully-formed taste buds,
but this sense starts developing only over the next
year, as they start trying different flavours.

TASTE IS GENERATED through a combination of taste and smell and even touch, once a baby starts to appreciate textures. It also involves a complex set of chemical reactions transmitting signals to the brain so that flavour can be experienced.

THE ANATOMY OF TASTE

Taste buds – formed during the 14th week of pregnancy – are a collection of cells that do the body's major sensory-processing work. Most are spread over the tongue in the tiny "taste papillae" bumps, but they're also found in the mouth, throat, and nose. Babies and small children also have them in the hard palate in the roof of the mouth, and the middle of the tongue, as well as the lips and cheeks.

NEW TASTES

In the first few months of life, all that a baby tastes is sweet milk – and there is evidence that the liking for sweet things may be inbuilt. A "sweet tooth" may be a biological mechanism to ensure that babies keep breastfeeding, and prefer calorie-packed food.

However, as a baby grows and her diet needs to be more varied, so does her ability to enjoy different tastes. This seems to be a mix of universal preferences – for instance, all babies seem to develop a liking for salt at

> New studies suggest that we also have receptors for fat, which would make it the sixth taste.

around four months – and learning to like new tastes. There is a "window of opportunity" in the first year of life, during which babies have wide preferences and will quite happily try new things. It's no coincidence that when they start moving around, at about one year, they start to develop neophobia, a fear of new experiences – including tastes – which peaks between 18 months and three years. The neophobic phase does have its evolutionary uses – it protects small children from eating things which might make them ill, or even kill them. In some ways, the sense of taste of small children is basic – as if they were still foragers. For example, bitter and sour tastes, which are unpleasant to a baby, can signal poisoned or rotten food. Equally, an attraction to sweet and salty tastes means that babies are programmed to eat carbohydrates, and therefore get the necessary level of salt and energy. However, this can be a problem because modern diets are packed with unnaturally high levels of sugar and salt.

SUPERTASTERS

Some babies have more taste papillae than average, and will grow up to be "supertasters", with a very sensitive sense of taste. More than 50 per cent of the population in India qualify as supertasters, as opposed to between 10 and 20 per cent of people in Japan and China.

BABY FACTS

As part of a self-protection mechanism, babies are born with an aversion to chilli as well as to bitter foods.

Sweet foods, such as carrot or jam, are initially preferred by babies. However, this liking for sweet tastes lessens with age as other flavours are tried and begin to be appreciated.

Salty tastes seem to develop in babies who are between three and six months old. However, some research shows that at first babies are indifferent to the taste of salt in water.

SOUR

SWEET

SALTY

BITTER

UMAMI

Bitter tastes, such as rocket, are unfamiliar and many babies have an instinctive aversion. The back of the tongue is more sensitive to bitter foods, possibly to provide a last-minute mechanism for sensing and spitting out toxic foods before swallowing them.

Umami is known as the fifth taste, along with the other basic tastes of salty, sweet, sour, and bitter. It has a savoury, meaty taste, and is found in Parmesan cheese, soy sauce, and bacon.

Sour foods, such as lemon, trigger a natural aversion in babies. A dislike of sour taste may be a result of a primal instinct that identifies sour and bitter tastes as potentially harmful.

What's that smell?

Although a young baby has blurry vision and imperfect hearing, her sense of smell is sharp, making this sense one of the most important in early life.

A VERY YOUNG BABY can't see her mother clearly, but she does know her scent, so even with her eyes closed, she can be reassured that she's protected, and close to milk. But it isn't only the smell of her own mother, or breast milk, that a young baby recognizes. The cells that respond to odour molecules lie high in the chambers of her nose, and allow her to detect and discriminate between a wide range of odours. The key developments over the next few years will be in her ability to match different smells to their sources – a skill acquired through experience and learning – and in her likes and dislikes.

{ Newborns have a highly developed sense of smell, even before their first bite of food! }

BAD ODOUR

Babies aged under a month old seem to have a built-in dislike of certain "bad" smells, such as butyric acid, commonly found in vomit. However, one of the challenges in determining what smells babies like and don't like is that not all scents are just scents. Some smelly compounds – menthol, for example – activate not only the odour-detecting cells in the nose, but also nerve endings that are sensitive to temperature (menthol activates "cold" sensors) and pain. A baby may be responding to these other sensations, not the smell itself.

By the time they reach eight to 12 months, most babies avoid a wide range of food odours that an adult would also wrinkle his nose at, but they are still wary of smells that most adults like. In one study, seven- to 15-month-olds spent less time chewing or handling an object scented with an odour that was unfamiliar to them, such as violet, even if that odour was rated as pleasant by adults. Other research with eight- to 12-month-olds found that they avoided a wide range of food smells that adults find unappealing, such as fishy, cabbage-like and sulphurous smells. However, they were not keen on fruity smells, which adults do generally like. This was also the case for 22-month-olds, suggesting it takes years for adult-like scent preferences to fully develop.

PAST SCENTS

One study aimed to test how good babies were at remembering smells. The infants learned to make an overhead mobile move (by kicking their legs) when a floral or woody smell was present, and later tested with the smells kept the same, or switched. The findings showed that three-month-old babies had a better memory for the smells than six-month-olds, suggesting that the sense of smell is more important in younger babies. However, after three days, both the three- and six-month-olds had forgotten connections that they had previously learned. Although scents seem to be good at bringing back long-lost memories in adults, the same doesn't seem to be true for babies.

BABY FACTS

A mother's scent is the most important smell for a young baby, and it helps to create the bond between them.

Fragrant flower Young babies take a while to acquire a liking for the same scents that most adults enjoy, such as a flower scent. So this baby may be more interested in the flower's pretty colour than its sweet smell.

Scented mint Babies generally dislike unfamiliar smells and tastes, so the fresh smell of mint is unlikely to appeal to most of them – unless it's familiar because it is used a lot at home.

BABY FACTS

Proteins are released in the vapour from fish and seafood during cooking. If inhaled by babies with a seafood allergy, it can trigger a dangerous reaction.

Vanilla Some experts think that babies like sweet smells, such as vanilla, but this is disputed. Adults across all cultures generally like vanilla, both as a flavour and a smell, but babies don't seem to be so sure about it.

Babies who had lavender-scented oil added to their bath cried less and slept more deeply afterwards, according to an American study. But researchers found that the mothers were also more relaxed, and touched their infants more during the bath. So it's not clear if the aroma relaxed the babies, or if it was the effect of the more relaxed mums.

Strong-smelling cheese When starting on solids, babies usually accept a wide range of foods, and some may enjoy the smell and taste of a few tiny cubes of a mature cheese.

Growing and learning

Watch me grow

From a tiny baby weighing an average of around three kilograms to a walking, inquisitive toddler, babies grow an incredible amount during their first few months.

IN THE FIRST YEAR OF LIFE, babies grow very fast, typically doubling their body weight between birth and their fifth month, and nearly trebling it by the time they are a year old. Parents and health professionals are often keen to keep track of this weight gain, to check that the baby's growth is "normal".

In recent years, the charts used for tracking baby weight have been changed and updated. The new charts, produced by the World Health Organization, reflect more accurately the slower, yet completely healthy, growth rate of babies who are solely breastfed. While the new charts are reassuring to parents whose babies are on the lighter side, they also reveal that more babies may be slightly overweight.

In fact, weight gain in babies can be affected by a number of factors, including of course the height and size of their parents. Shorter than average parents with healthy babies will often see weight gain on the low side of the charts, while babies with tall parents will typically progress along the higher side.

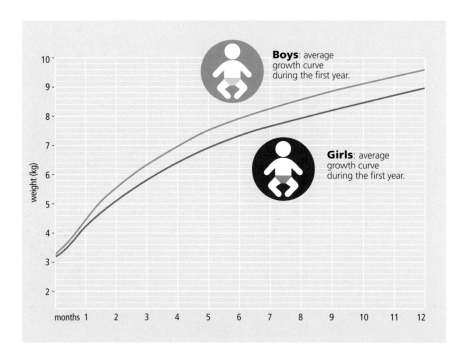

Boys: average growth curve during the first year.

Girls: average growth curve during the first year.

Growth chart (left) This shows a slow, steady increase in weight in baby boys and girls. Boys tend to grow faster than girls.

Height (below) The average baby grows approximately 24cm (9in) during the first year. If a baby continued to grow at this extraordinary rate, she'd be almost 5m (16ft) tall by the time she reached adulthood.

During their first year, babies grow at an amazing rate, both in terms of their height and their weight. While this growth will naturally differ from baby to baby, most babies will have trebled their birth weight by the time they reach a year old.

BABY'S AVERAGE WEIGHT
At birth, she'll be around one-third of her weight at one year.

BABY'S AVERAGE WEIGHT
At five months, she will almost double her birth weight.

BABY'S AVERAGE WEIGHT
At one year, she is about three times her weight at birth.

Growing facts

Babies usually grow in a predictable way, but even a healthy baby may gain or lose weight unexpectedly. However, it is more important that the trend on the growth charts continues upwards.

Babies go from being helpless to independent movement in 12 months!

The first milk from the breast is low in fat, so the baby can lose up to **10%** of her body weight after birth.

Fully nutritious breast milk does not arrive until **2–3** days after the birth.

By **2** weeks later, **80%** of babies have regained their birth weight.

LOSING AND GAINING

Immediately after birth, almost all babies lose weight—typically about five to seven percent of their body weight following birth, even in healthy babies. This is very normal, and in fact is something that the baby has already prepared for: her last four weeks in the womb were spent putting on body fat. The drop in weight is a natural occurrence, partly due to the fact that the milk is not, at this stage, high in fat. Later it will change, and be thicker and creamier.

NATURAL DROP

Because, after birth, a mother's breast milk is thinner and more watery than more mature milk, the baby has to survive on body fat, plus the colostrum that her mum produces in the first couple of days. The hormone (prolactin) that causes milk production is activated after the placenta is delivered, and the first milk that the baby receives is already present in the breast at birth. As a baby breast-feeds, the fat content increases over time.

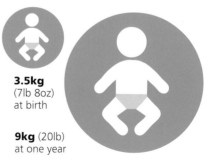

3.5kg (7lb 8oz) at birth

9kg (20lb) at one year

FACT

The average weight of a newborn in Western countries tends to be about 3.5kg (7lb 8oz). By the time children reach one year old, the average is around 9kg (20lb).

SIZE AND SHAPE

Babies' body proportions are very different than those of adults: they have proportionately much bigger heads, and an extended middle section, or torso. Because of this, the growth and development of a baby's skeleton doesn't take place uniformly. The bones of a baby's arms and legs grow faster than those in the skull or torso. This pattern continues through childhood until puberty.

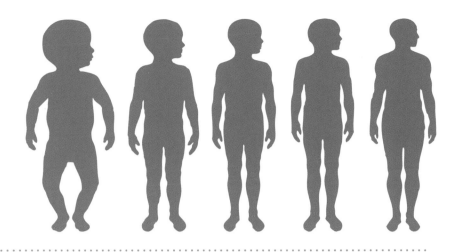

ORDER OF MILK TEETH

When a baby is born, all the first or "milk" teeth are present in the gums and are waiting to grow. The first teeth migrate from around three or four months, although babies differ as to the age when their first teeth show. Symptoms of teething, such as dribbling, chewing, loose stools, and red cheeks, can start a long time before the tooth eventually erupts.

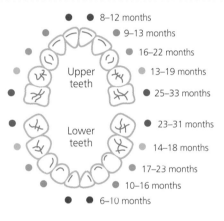

8–12 months
9–13 months
16–22 months
Upper teeth
13–19 months
25–33 months
Lower teeth
23–31 months
14–18 months
17–23 months
10–16 months
6–10 months

Order of appearance of milk teeth: Upper and lower incisors; upper and lower lateral incisors; upper and lower first molars; upper and lower canines; then finally, the upper and lower second molars.

- central incisor
- lateral incisor
- canine
- first molar
- second molar

HANDS AND FEET

During a baby's first few years, her foot does not contain any fully formed bones. Instead, it's made from soft, flexible cartilage, surrounded by fatty tissue— this is what makes babies' feet so plump and soft. The arches are undefined and the toes are all similar lengths. Babies have a greater range of movement in their feet than when they are older—they use them more like hands, sometimes trying to grip things with hands and feet at the same time.

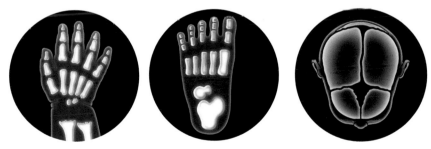

Bendy bones In babies up to one year old, the bones in the hands and feet are made of a soft, pliable cartilage. These flexible bones start to harden, fuse together, and become much more solid as the baby grows, and begins to stand upright. Wrist bone formation does not start until the infant is three years old; it will be fully formed by the age of 18 to 20.

FACT

Babies are born with two fontanelles (soft spots) on their heads. These allow the skull to stretch as the brain grows, and close during childhood.

Glorious food
Getting to grips with it

A newborn baby survives purely on milk; 12 months later she is sitting up to a full meal. How do babies manage this progression?

BABIES ARE BORN with the sucking and rooting reflex, and, at first, this is all they need as the only food for a tiny baby is, of course, milk. Up to the age of six months, a baby's system cannot cope with complex foods, and all the energy and nutrients she requires are provided through an exclusive diet of either breast milk, which is recommended by the World Health Organization, or formula. By the age of six months, the baby is growing fast and her body is beginning to require additional nutrients – and this is when the process of introducing solid foods begins.

WAITING TO MATURE

This recommendation to stick with exclusive milk feeding up to the age of six months applies worldwide, including in countries where hygiene and sterilizing standards are immaculate. This is because physically and developmentally babies need to mature to a point where they are ready to move onto "solid" (normal) food – and this applies equally to babies who start off with particularly low or high birth weights: it's about maturity, not size.

All babies need time to develop the right levels of enzymes to enable them to efficiently digest the proteins, fats, and carbohydrates present in normal foods. They also need sufficient time for the digestive system to mature to the point when it can cope with foods other than milk, as the baby could develop an allergic reaction or a gut infection from a food that has been introduced into her system too early. However, after six months a baby's digestive system has developed sufficiently to be able to effectively process all the essential extra nutrients that her body now requires – in particular, iron – but which cannot be provided from milk or formula alone.

SAFE PICKERS

Very young children put almost anything in their mouths, to touch as well as to taste. By the age of two, though, many children develop some form of "neophobia" – dislike and fear of anything new, including foods. Evolution experts believe that this is a defence mechanism. Children avoid trying unfamiliar foods, which may be dangerous, especially if their curiosity leads them to venture away from mum.

CHANGING FACES

Also at around six months, the bottom half of a baby's face changes shape, with the jaw growing bigger and the fat pads in the cheeks reducing a little bit. It may not be perceptible (most six-month-olds still have very round, chubby faces) but these changes mean a baby is now able to fit food into her mouth, move her tongue around, and chew properly.

ALL SYSTEMS GO

Other mechanisms and reflexes develop at the same time, enabling a baby to acquire the physical coordination to pick up and – most importantly – swallow food. These mechanisms include the ability to

FROM LIQUIDS TO SOLIDS

Breast milk and infant formula both provide a baby with a wholesome and nutritious diet for the first six months of life. The transition from milk to solids is a messy and experimental stage, with some babies preferring to feed themselves, while others are happy to be fed by an adult.

Primitive reflex
One of a baby's earliest urges is to suck, and on contact with a nipple or the teat of a bottle, this reflex is instinctively activated, enabling the baby to feed.

Breast milk
Thirst-quenching breast milk is made up of 90 per cent water, and is filled with key nutrients, such as proteins, minerals, and sugar, which will satisfy a baby's hunger. Breast milk also provides the baby with essential enzymes, useful bacteria, hormones, growth factors, and antibodies.

Formula
Designed as a nutritious alternative to breast milk, infant formula is usually derived from cow's milk. Formula contains many energy-providing nutrients, including carbohydrates, proteins, unsaturated fats, vitamins, and minerals. However, unlike breast milk, it does not contain antibodies.

> Babies need, and actually seem to prefer, carbohydrates rather than other sorts of food.

HAND TO MOUTH
A baby's instinct to put food – or anything else! – in her mouth is what encourages the success of self-feeding. Even if a baby hasn't got teeth, chunks of food, such as bread, can be sucked.

SPOON-FED
Once a baby has lost her natural inclination to reject foreign objects from her mouth, she is ready to accept food from a spoon. This is the basis of traditional weaning.

FIRST FORMULA

The first infant formula – a mix of cow's milk, wheat and malt flour, and potassium bicarbonate – went on sale in the 1860s. It was developed by one of the leading German chemists of the day, Justus von Liebig. The formula was initially made in liquid form, and then was later powdered as it kept for longer.

WELCOME TO FOOD

The traditional "okuizome", or "first eating", ceremony in Japan is held when a baby is 100 days old. The baby is too little to eat, but the ceremony is to hope she never goes hungry. Sea bream, umeboshi plums, and sticky red rice are served, and a stone – which no one eats, but is there to symbolize strong teeth for the baby.

INDIAN BABY RICE

The Hindu ceremony "annaprashana", or "first rice", is conducted when a baby is around six months old. To begin with, the baby is fed mashed rice or rice pudding as a first food. Then, the baby picks up a book, a bangle, a pen, or a pot – to symbolize her future direction in life.

sit upright and hold up her head, and the development of enough fine motor skills to be able to grasp and hold food. In addition, the automatic rooting and sucking reflexes of a milk-fed newborn disappear, and now instead of pushing any food straight back out of the mouth, a baby can hold it in and swallow it without choking. The timespan for these developments varies, but, give or take a week or two, they broadly take place at around six months.

FIRST FOODS

Usually at this stage, a baby is ready to move on to solid foods, although, for the first few months, most of her calories still come from milk. Initially, food is more for play and experimentation than for actual nutrition. There are two main styles of introducing solids to a baby – "traditional" weaning and "baby-led" weaning.

Traditional weaning is when a baby is fed puréed fruits or vegetables, often mixed in with baby rice and milk, and spooned into the mouth by an adult. Baby-led weaning, or "self-feeding", is when the baby picks up the food and eats it without any help. Hard foods, such as apples or carrots, which are easy to choke on might be softened through cooking, but broadly speaking self-feeding means eating the same sorts of "family foods" as adults.

Some studies suggest that babies who self-feed have a lower risk of obesity later in life, as they learn to regulate their own food intake from the beginning, and eat only when they are hungry and stop when they've had enough.

FROM MILK TO SOLIDS

MILK provides all the nutrients a baby needs for the first six months.

WEANING involves introducing solid foods in addition to all the normal milk feeds.

A VARIED DIET involves eating a balance of protein, fats, vegetables, fruits, carbohydrates, and dairy.

> *… the automatic rooting and sucking reflexes of a milk-fed newborn disappear… instead of pushing any food straight back out of the mouth, a baby can hold it in and swallow it without choking.*

Eating for beginners

Once a baby is used to eating solids, a wide range of foods can be offered. Extending her palate at an early stage can help to prevent fussy eating later on.

Fats and oils
Essential fatty acids, including omega-3 and omega-6, are needed for brain development and vision, and are found, primarily, in oily fish.

Meat and fish
Lean red meat is a good – and the most easily absorbed – source of iron. Chicken and fish provide protein, and oily fish, such as salmon, help development of the brain and nervous system.

Dairy foods
Full-fat dairy produce, such as yoghurt and cheese, provide essential vitamins and fats, and are a good source of calcium.

Starchy foods
These foods, such as rice, pasta, grains, and potatoes, are the most common type of carbohydrate and provide babies with an important source of energy.

Fruits and vegetables
A baby needs five small portions daily, including green vegetables, such as broccoli, yellow and orange vegetables, such as carrots or sweet potato, and a little fruit.

fats and oils · *dairy foods* · *starchy foods* · *fruits and vegetables* · *meat and fish*

IF AT FIRST YOU DON'T SUCCEED...

In a successful study that aimed to boost the amount of vegetables in the diet of a group of 450 toddlers, researchers found that...

TRY...
... children who tasted a new fruit or vegetable at least 10 times...

TRY...
... showed a 61 per cent increase in their liking of that food...

AGAIN!
... and the amount of the vegetable that they would eat trebled.

> *Food is more than just fuel. It's also a central part of every culture… and babies… learn to eat by example.*

SIZE ISN'T EVERYTHING, and when it comes to baby and toddler nutrition, a "little and often" approach is the key. Children require broadly the same healthy diet as adults, but with a few important twists.

QUALITY NOT QUANTITY

Babies have much smaller stomachs than adults, so they don't need vast quantities at any one meal, but what they do need is nutritional balance. Too much fibre, for example, fills them up without giving them the full range of nutrients they need. And while the global obesity crisis has focused negative attention on the fat in childrens' diets, babies and toddlers need to be fuelled up. They don't need extra sugar or fry-ups, but eating good fats is important. "We need some fats, for healthy skin and nerve function – in particular, the omega-3 oils from oily fish", points out British Dietetic Association spokesperson Azmina Govindji. "Dairy is very important, too, at this age, because small children need the calcium." They also need snacks to keep their systems ticking over.

Most nutrients can be sourced directly from food, but not always in sufficient quantities. In Europe and North America, for example, concerns over low levels of vitamin D in children have lead to certain medical associations recommending giving children supplements to cover any gaps in their diet.

EATING BY EXAMPLE

Food is more than just fuel. It's also a central part of every culture and sub-culture, and human babies, like those of most other species, learn to eat by example. They note very early on what sorts of food are being eaten around them, and are far more likely to eat something they have seen another human eat in front of them.

In this way, babies learn to eat what is familiar, but they can also learn to recognize and feel comfortable with an extensive range of foods. Babies accustomed to eating many different foods from weaning onwards are less likely to be fussy eaters later on, because their palates have been widened at an early stage.

IRON RATIONS

Iron is an essential mineral that many toddlers lack; it enables red blood cells to carry oxygen around the body. Babies are born with a reserve of iron.

 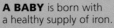

A BABY is born with a healthy supply of iron.

BY 6 MONTHS, iron levels start to drop.

EATING IRON RICH foods will rebalance this.

BABY'S RED CELLS are replenished.

Building up defences

Babies have an amazing ability to protect themselves
from germs in their environment that can cause infection.
But this immunity to infection takes time to develop.

WE RELY ON OUR IMMUNE SYSTEM to protect us from infection; however, a baby's immunity isn't fully developed for some time. The immune system is a complex network that comprises bone marrow, hormones, white blood cells, antibodies, organs, such as the thymus and spleen, and also the lymphatic system. The lymphatic system is the body's drainage network: its main job is to return fluid from tissues back to the blood, but it also acts as a transport network for white blood cells and antibodies. Like many of the body's systems, it takes time to reach maturity.

GETTING THE SYSTEM GOING

Until a baby's immune system has developed, she needs some protection from infection. Babies receive some antibodies directly from their mother during the last three months of pregnancy, and after birth through colostrum and breast milk – a process called "passive immunity". These antibodies are primed and ready for action as soon as the baby gets them, but exactly which antibodies the baby receives through passive immunity will depend on the specific germs her mother has already been exposed to. Antibodies are classified into five different types, each with different roles. Only one type of antibody is passed across to the baby through the placenta during pregnancy. However, all five types are present in breast milk and transfer to the baby.

From around two to three months old, a healthy baby begins to generate her own antibodies – her "active immunity". Antibodies are produced by the body following exposure to germs, and they bind to the invading bacteria, making them inactive. So if a baby comes into contact with germs, for example by eating something from the floor, this helps to develop her immune system.

A HELPING HAND

Vaccines mimic a specific germ that is capable of causing infection. They trick the immune system into reacting as if it has been exposed to a potential threat. It then responds by producing antibodies to that particular infection, providing the baby with long-term immunity.

Babies are at high risk of contracting infections, so administering vaccines at an early age – even before the immune system has fully developed – is important. Vaccinations can be given from around two months of age, and are effective in boosting a baby's immune system so that they can avoid some of the more dangerous childhood diseases. The importance of baby vaccinations is recognized worldwide, with different countries implementing their own schedules.

Newborn

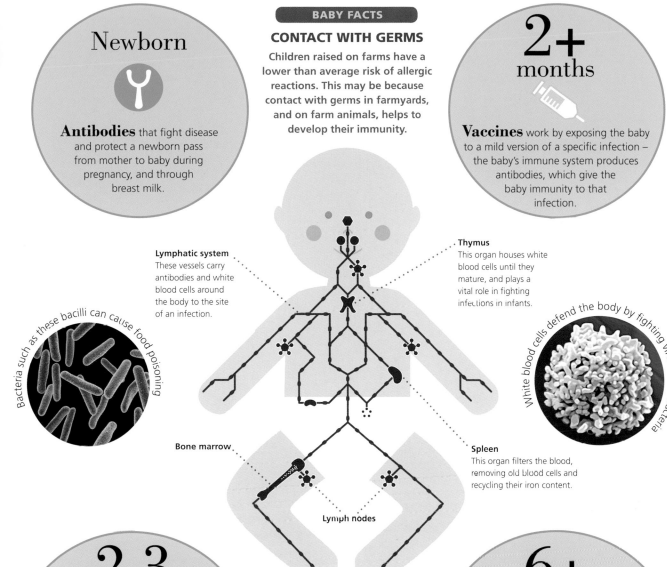

Antibodies that fight disease and protect a newborn pass from mother to baby during pregnancy, and through breast milk.

BABY FACTS

CONTACT WITH GERMS

Children raised on farms have a lower than average risk of allergic reactions. This may be because contact with germs in farmyards, and on farm animals, helps to develop their immunity.

2+ months

Vaccines work by exposing the baby to a mild version of a specific infection – the baby's immune system produces antibodies, which give the baby immunity to that infection.

Lymphatic system
These vessels carry antibodies and white blood cells around the body to the site of an infection.

Thymus
This organ houses white blood cells until they mature, and plays a vital role in fighting infections in infants.

Bacteria such as these bacilli can cause food poisoning

White blood cells defend the body by fighting viruses and bacteria

Bone marrow

Spleen
This organ filters the blood, removing old blood cells and recycling their iron content.

Lymph nodes

2-3 months

Antibodies can now be produced by the baby in response to exposure to germs.

BABY FACTS

CAN HOMES BE TOO CLEAN?

The answer is complicated: while some evidence clearly supports this idea, dropping our hygiene standards would also mean that infections are more likely.

6+ months

The immune system, including cells, hormones, and bone marrow, is now active and continues to mature and protect the baby from infection.

Getting stronger

As a baby grows, her muscles need to get stronger to
support her, and to enable her to practise all
the new movements she needs to explore her world.

DURING A BABY'S first few weeks, her muscle control is weak and uncoordinated. This is because movement within her mother's womb has been limited, and all those tiny muscles have yet to start working to their full potential. As muscles start to be used, however, she gains more control, leading to more purposeful, fluid movements. In just a few months she will have transformed into an energetic and coordinated little person.

HEADS UP

At one month, a baby should be able to support her own head when she is being held upright, and to lift her head from a lying position for very short intervals of time. By two months, this has improved and she can hold up her head for longer periods. By four months, she can keep her head upright much of the time when sitting or being held. By four or five months, the ability to turn over kicks in, and she starts rolling – one side is usually favoured at first, but later she will be able to roll in either direction.

STARTING TO SIT

Babies learn to sit at different times – some start from as young as four months. To be able to sit, they must have several other building blocks of motor development in place – they should be able to hold up the head, have a degree of balance, and have started to develop muscles in the back and torso. At first, if you sit a baby on the floor unsupported, she is able to sit for a few seconds before toppling over to one side or the other. Gradually, her sense of balance and the strength of her back muscles increase, although she will often sit angled forwards to aid with balance, with one or both hands on the floor (the "tripod" sit). By six or seven months old, she should be able to sit while being supported, and then progress to sitting unsupported. She will soon realize that it is much easier to see, play, and interact with her world when sitting up.

TUMMY TIME

Placing a baby on her front has benefits for physical development – extending the spine and limbs, and encouraging the baby to lift her head to see the world around her. This leads to increased strength in the neck, upper shoulder, and trunk muscles. Tummy time also helps with strength in the arms and shoulders, which helps with crawling later on and with pulling up to standing.

STANDING STRONG

At nine or ten months, a baby learns not just to stand, but to bend the knees and straighten them again. She will be able to stoop down to pick up a favourite toy, and to squat and get back up again with increasing fluidity. Initially, standing is likely to be achieved through pulling herself up with the aid of furniture, but soon, as her muscles develop, she will be doing it all on her own. A change also takes place in the feet at this stage and those pudgy, soft feet begin to take her weight and to grow stronger.

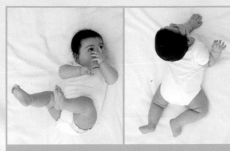

Back-to-front roll and head up

Strengthening her muscles As a baby's muscles improve in strength and coordination, they prepare her for the next stage of development – so in a just few months she progresses from rolling, to sitting, to getting ready to crawl.

{ Rolling over is one thing – but rolling back to where she came from is quite another! }

Starting to sit unsupported

Getting stronger month by month

Every physical developmental milestone is a step
along the way to full coordination.

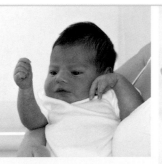

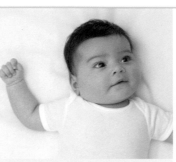

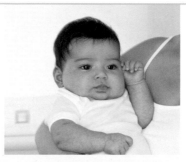

1 MONTH
• Lifts head and can
hold it at an angle
• Can wave arms and
kick legs
• Can grasp objects

2 MONTHS
• Can turn head to follow
objects
• Can hold up head for
short periods
• Can bear weight on legs

3 MONTHS
• Can hold head steady
for longer
• Can make smooth
movements of limbs
• Can "stand" when held up
• May be able to lift head and
shoulders from lying flat

4 MONTHS
• May be able to push up
head and shoulders
• Begins rolling over
• Can hold head up for
long periods

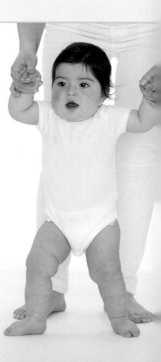

9 MONTHS
• Can stand better
• Picks up objects
between thumb
and fingers
• Cruises around
more confidently

10 MONTHS
• Can wave on request
• Picks up objects with
improved skill
• Can stand alone for short
periods
• Places objects in pots

She will soon realize that it is much easier to see, play, and interact with her world when sitting up.

5 MONTHS
- Can roll over, usually in just one direction
- May start to sit if supported

6 MONTHS
- May start to prepare for crawling
- Can turn towards sounds
- May sit unaided
- Can roll in both directions

7 MONTHS
- Can sit without support
- Can move with smoother movements
- Starts to crawl, or is preparing to crawl
- May start to stand, with support, and move ("cruise")

8 MONTHS
- Begins to crawl well
- Can pass objects between hands
- Can stand holding on to furniture, and cruises around more
- Can point and wave

11 MONTHS
- Stands unsupported for longer
- Can place shapes in correct containers
- Can bend down while standing

12 MONTHS
- Can indicate object she wants
- Starts to take some steps
- Walking begins

14–18 MONTHS
- Can walk with the support of a push-along toy
- May walk backwards
- May tackle stairs, with help
- May be able to dance and take small running steps

12–14 MONTHS
- Can walk a couple of steps unaided, with toes turned out; may walk on tiptoe
- Uses arms to keep balance

19–24 MONTHS
- May be able to run
- Can hold an item while walking
- May jump from low objects, such as a step
- Stair-ability improves

Starting to explore

As babies grow and develop, they begin to explore their surroundings. While this is very exciting for babies, it brings a new feeling of vulnerability as they start to stray from the safety of their parents.

ONCE BABIES become more mobile, they enter a phase of actively learning more about their world by exploring it and acquiring new skills. There are no perfect toys for this; babies seem to be happy playing with anything that attracts their curiosity, and that they can handle and carefully examine.

HAND JIVE

Even before babies can use their hands, they are fascinated by them. They seem to bring their hands in front of their face deliberately, so that they can explore their own movements by watching them. This may be how a baby learns to identify a movement as her own – by noticing the match between what she sees, and the sensations she feels when she watches her own hands move.

?

EARLY EXPLORERS CLEVER KIDS

Early exploration has far-reaching consequences: babies who explore a lot at five months old, are likely to perform better than those who don't on a whole host of intelligence tests as teenagers. This might be because a baby who explores more gives herself more opportunities to learn.

SITTING COMFORTABLY

Once babies can sit up by themselves, usually at around five or six months, they suddenly seem to understand a lot more about objects – they are able to recognize them from different perspectives, and even to remember their textures and patterns. Babies also seem to understand that things will fall down if they are not supported.

The reason for this change might be that, while a baby is still learning to sit up, the effort of trying to remain upright takes up much of her attention. Once she can sit up easily and securely, she not only has more opportunities to explore now her hands are free, but she can also devote more of her attention to the things she is playing with.

They're mine! For a newborn, hands are fascinating toys and an endless source of interest, especially when the baby realizes they belong to her!

> *Throw off the bowlines, sail away from the safe harbour, catch the trade wind in your sails. Explore. Dream. Discover.*
>
> **Mark Twain (1835–1910)**

Stack them up Playing with stacking cups helps a baby to work out how things relate to each other, and to learn action (push) and consequence (fall down)!

50% of babies can walk by one year.

BABIES AGED 9 MONTHS 96% can sit up without any support, 92% can crawl.

MOVING EXPERIENCE

Being able to move around independently also has a profound effect on the way that babies experience their environment. Scientists have discovered that a fear of heights emerges once babies become mobile.

It's also at about this age when babies develop another fear: wariness of new people and new things. Before eight months, babies will touch anything offered to them, with little hesitation, but from around this age they become much more discerning. One plausible explanation is that, if a baby has wandered off and mum isn't there to protect her, being wary about new things might be a sensible precaution.

Natural caution Stranger anxiety is a natural development for a baby, and should disappear in time. It sometimes happens because the baby now understands the difference between her mum and a stranger – and prefers mum!

Discovering for yourself Given an unfamiliar toy, a baby will examine it carefully from all angles. Then he will work out how to dismantle it – and possibly how to put it back together!

Exploring together Babies seem quite companionable sitting near each other, but until the age of two they are still exploring individually in parallel play, rather than together.

Reaching out Now her muscles are strong enough, she can pull herself up to reach out for her toy. Once she has managed this, her confidence will grow and soon she will be standing without support.

{ *Babies with an older sibling explore more when their older sibling is around, and will stray further from their parents.* }

Sisterly help A baby's older sister can hold her, and help her to learn how to play with toys.

EXPLORING AND RETURNING TO BASE

Learning to crawl seems to cement a baby's attachment to her parents. She might crawl off to explore something that looks enticing and suddenly realize that mum is not at her side anymore. Parents then represent a secure base from which a baby can go off and explore her world, while knowing she can return to safety. Parents report that when their babies start crawling, they seem to be more sensitive to their parents' comings and goings, but also more affectionate.

Out of sight, out of mind
Hidden object

DISCOVERING THE SCIENCE

1   **OBJECT HIDDEN UNDER A CLOTH**   The baby is at first interested only in the blue cloth that covers the toy duck.

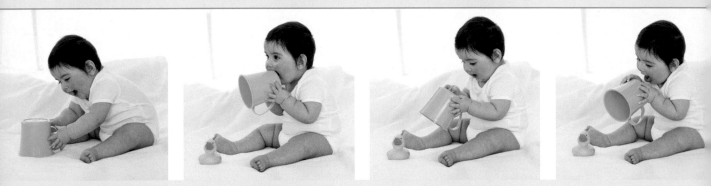

2   **OBJECT HIDDEN UNDER AN OPAQUE POT**   Again, the bright blue pot is examined, not the toy beneath.

3   **OBJECT UNDER A TRANSPARENT CONTAINER**   The container is see-through, so she spots the toy at once.

Before they are seven months old, babies won't try to find a toy they've seen being hidden. This is because they don't fully understand that an object still exists even when they can't actually see it.

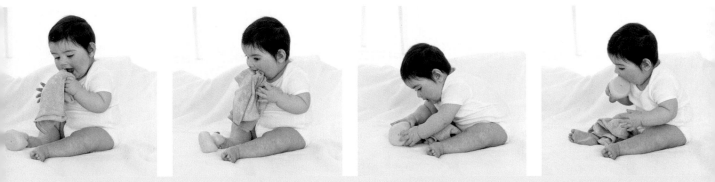

Once the cloth has been tasted, it is set aside, then she notices the toy underneath and tests it by chewing it.

Once she notices the object, she moves the pot away and concentrates on the duck, examining it carefully.

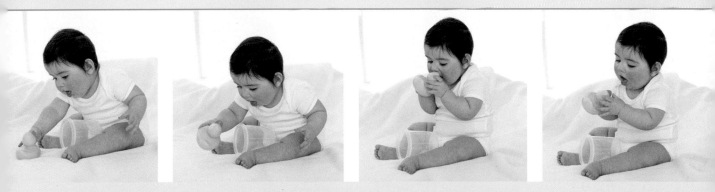

The container is immediately discarded and forgotten because the toy is now of more interest to her.

Getting around

Once babies start to become stronger, the transition from being an immobile newborn to being an active and inquisitive toddler happens quite quickly. All too soon, she's cruising around the furniture – and then, taking her first couple of steps.

Coordinating limbs Essential to crawling is the baby's ability to coordinate her legs and arms to move in contrary motion – moving opposite arms and legs. Months of rolling, kicking, and lying on her tummy gradually build up the requisite muscles to enable this new means of transport.

ONE OF THE MOST EXCITING – and potentially nerve-wracking – times of a parent's life with a new baby is when she becomes mobile. Initially shuffling or crawling across the room, she gradually builds up her strength and balance until she can toddle along, unaided. It's a time of immense change for a baby, both physically and in terms of her experience of the world.

CRAWLING

It all starts at around six to eight months, when a baby starts to get to grips with crawling – although some babies bypass the crawling stage altogether, going from a "bum-shuffle" straight to toddling.

A baby's first step towards crawling is when she makes little "push-up" movements with her hands to raise her head and shoulders off the floor. This increases her strength, and from this movement she progresses to kneeling on all fours, and eventually to locomotion. Coordination is key with crawling: the act of putting one hand, and the opposite knee, forwards. Practice leads to greater ability – and the impetus to keep going.

CRAWLING AROUND THE WORLD

Some cultures don't encourage crawling – possibly to reduce a baby's exposure to potential pathogens on the ground. The Au hunter-gatherer tribe of Papua New Guinea, for example, carry their babies until they can walk – when not on a parent's back, a baby is placed on the ground in a sitting, not crawling, position.

 He who would learn to fly one day must first learn to stand and walk and run and climb and dance; one cannot fly into flying.

Friedrich Nietzsche (1844–1900)

Early push-up movements A crucial development on the path to mobility is building up strength by lying on the tummy and

Shuffling to the side commando style The comical "commando crawl" – when the baby hauls herself along on her tummy

Sliding along the floor towards a toy The incentive of a toy to crawl towards is often a good motivator for a baby to get going!

DO THE SHUFFLE

Some babies have amusing methods of getting around that can't strictly be called crawling – from the "commando crawl" (dragging themselves across the floor with their arms) to the "bum shuffle" (sitting on one side of their bottom and sliding along the floor). Some babies initially go sideways or backwards, rather than forwards, but all methods are completely normal, and continue the necessary muscle development that prepares them for the ultimate goal of walking.

PULLING UP AND CRUISING

Between their seventh and tenth month, babies reach the next stage of mobility: pulling themselves up to standing, using an adult or furniture for support. From this point, a baby soon develops the ability to "cruise" around the room by holding onto furniture, well before she can walk unaided. Her feet may curve under at this stage, as she has not yet learned to stretch out her toes, but as her foot lengthens the toes will spread out and splay a little, helping control her balance.

raising the head; from here it is a short step to rising onto all fours.

TIRED OUT?
Many parents hope that once their baby starts to crawl, this increase in her daily exercise will mean she sleeps better at night. However, a study in 2013 at Israel's University of Haifa suggests that, in fact, babies who are crawling are prone to be more restless at night, and to wake more often. Not ideal news for parents!

with one arm – often precedes proper crawling.

> *Some babies initially go sideways or backwards, rather than forwards, but all methods are completely normal…*

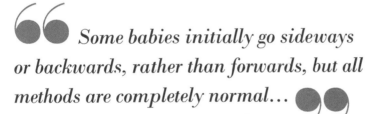

Pulling herself up Even once she has gained sufficient strength to stand, her feet still need to develop and uncurl to support her weight.

FIRST STEPS

The progression to walking usually occurs between 10 and 15 months, although this varies from baby to baby. Many start to walk around the time of their first birthday.

At first, a baby tends to walk with her legs widely spaced, as her hips and legs have not yet moved into their final positions relative to the pelvis, and her hip joints are still somewhat in the "frog" position they retain from birth. Push-along toys can help at this stage, as they give her stability while allowing forward motion. She also learns to squat and stand up again at this stage, so she can pick up a toy she has dropped. As she gains better control of her limbs, her balance also develops to prevent her toppling over, and once she starts to walk, she holds her hands and arms out at the sides.

SOCIAL INTERACTIONS

The progression to walking also goes hand in hand with the development of social interactions between the baby and those around her. Once she can walk, she spends longer periods engaged in social activities, such as showing a toy to an adult and having an exchange about it. So, learning to walk is more than just a physical milestone – it's a key part of a baby's overall development.

EARLIER EQUALS SMARTER?
Walking early is considered by some to be a sign of intelligence, suggesting a child is more advanced than her peers who walk later. However, a study by scientists in Switzerland followed babies until they were 18 years old, and concluded that there is no link between early milestones, such as walking, and later development of intelligence and coordination.

Unsteady stand
Early attempts at standing help to build muscle and balance before she starts to move.

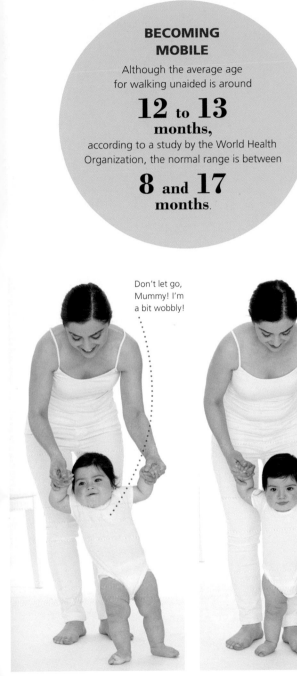

BECOMING MOBILE

Although the average age for walking unaided is around **12 to 13 months**, according to a study by the World Health Organization, the normal range is between **8 and 17 months**.

Don't let go, Mummy! I'm a bit wobbly!

Left, right, left, right, must keep going forwards…

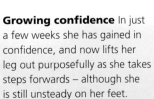

Hey everyone, check me out! I'm walking!

Balancing on mum Although upright, she leans heavily on mum, showing a wide gait. A combination of lack of balance, muscle control, and strength means that babies are often comically wobbly at this stage.

Growing confidence In just a few weeks she has gained in confidence, and now lifts her leg out purposefully as she takes steps forwards – although she is still unsteady on her feet.

Best foot forward Now she has better control of her limbs, and moves with a steady gait.

Getting a grip

To use her hands effectively, a baby must first develop hand-eye coordination. Moving constantly, and looking intensely at her hands, helps to establish connections between her brain, hands, and eyes.

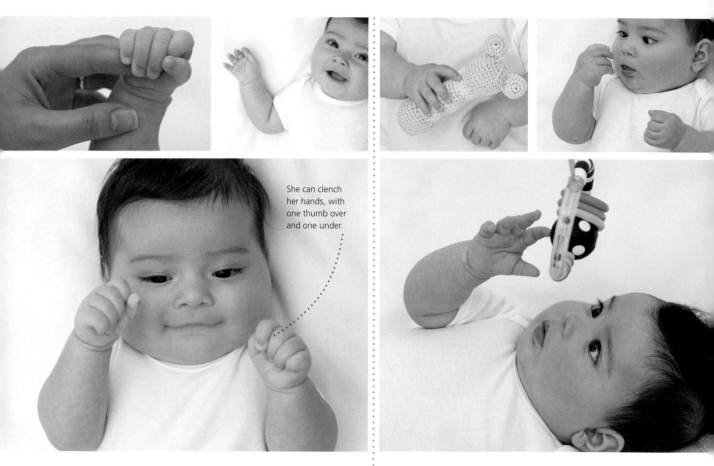

She can clench her hands, with one thumb over and one under.

0–2 MONTHS

A newborn who feels a finger in her palm will grab it as an involuntary reflex action. Her fingers may be clenched into a fist, with her thumb over or under her fingers. By two months, this reflex response has gone, and she can open and close her fingers at will. She watches her hands intently, learning to link what she feels to what she can see.

2–4 MONTHS

At about three months, a baby enjoys lying on her back and batting at objects above her. She may be able to reach for a toy and grab it in what's known as a "power grip" – with all four fingers clasping the object against the palm. Also, she starts to develop "pre-precision" grips, when the pads of her thumbs make contact with the pads of her index or middle fingers.

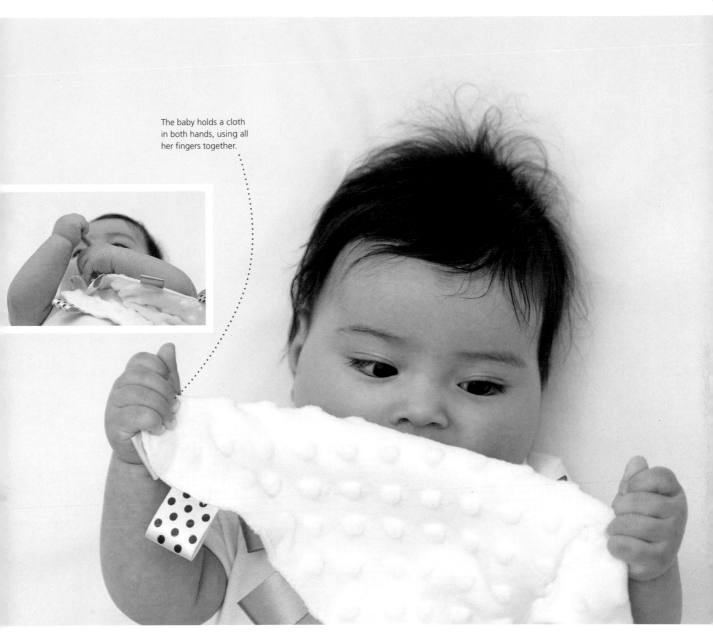

The baby holds a cloth in both hands, using all her fingers together.

4–6 MONTHS

A five-month-old can grasp an object, such as a teddy or a block, but is still using her thumb and fingers together, so she can't yet pick up a small object, such as a pea. At this age, she may grasp at herself, using one hand to grip the other, or to grab at her clothing. She can use a power grip to hold a piece of food, such as a rusk. As she learns to sit, she will start to reach for and manipulate toys.

Looking closely at the toy, she decides whether to use a finger or whole-hand grasp.

6–8 MONTHS

By now, a baby starts to use a precision or "pincer" grip, with thumb and forefinger together, to pick up tiny objects. She can estimate distance and size, and can plan what type of grip to use – power or pincer – in order to reach for an object without over- or under-shooting. She appears to use visual information about the texture of an object to plan which grasp to use.

66 ... She uses visual information about the texture of an object to plan what type of grasp to use... 99

A toy is held in each hand in a confident grip.

She can now try to use a cup with a double-handed grip.

8–10 MONTHS

At about nine months, she is able to hold a toy in each hand, and pass objects from one hand to another. She can prod objects with her index finger and drag them towards her. At this age, she enjoys holding things then dropping them onto the floor. Often, she closes her fingers just prior to contact with a toy she wants to pick up, rather than keeping them wide.

10–12 MONTHS PLUS

She can now reach for a toy, grasp it, and hold it, but she's still a long way from having refined capabilities. Many one-year-olds love "finger foods", which they can pick up and eat, but often a baby won't feed herself using a spoon or fork until she's around 18 months. It isn't until a child is about two that she can reliably use a normal cup without spilling the contents.

Grasping and holding

DIPS AND LEAPS

A four-week-old baby given a coloured rattle may extend her arm towards it, and even open her hand. At this age, her brain is using information from her eyes to direct the motion of her arms and hands. However, this simple form of reaching vanishes at six to seven weeks. It then reappears, in a more advanced form, at around five months. At this age, she can aim better and often can touch the object. Why the fluctuation in ability? Neuroscientists think it reflects a maturation and rewiring of the baby's brain: early "pre-reaching" is a pre-programmed pattern, which breaks down and is rebuilt as goal-directed, not conscious, reaching and grabbing.

HANDS AND FINGERS

Some researchers have found that improvements in a baby's ability to use her hands may be synchronized with vocal developments related to language. At two to four months, a baby begins to make cooing noises and learns how to move her fingers. These movements might be described as "hand babbling". Vocal babbling develops from about six to 10 months, when babies also make rhythmic motions of their hands. A baby's experiments with hand and finger movements are similar to her attempts to make new sounds, and in both cases, she seems to be learning to adopt techniques that are useful and to discard others. For deaf babies exposed to sign language, hand babbling is an essential building block for later language development.

FEEL THE FORCE

At first, when using the precision "pincer" grip, babies tend to go for more force than is necessary. This gives a stable grip, and it's less likely that she will drop the object, but there's more of a chance it will break. However, even a six-month-old baby varies the force used for grasping similar objects. Researchers think this is because her brain is trying out different strategies and patterns of movement, to work out the most effective. She'll need a wide-handed power grip for a solid ball that will fit in her hand, but a narrower pincer grip for a soft beanbag. At nine months, babies haven't learned that bigger objects are usually heavier, and need more force and a stronger grip. A 14-month-old, however, can learn to adjust their force and grip.

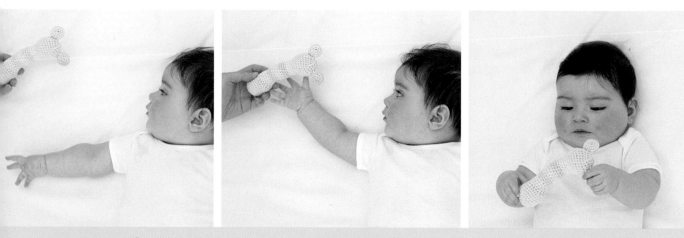

Stretching and reaching for a toy stops at six weeks, then reappears in a more advanced form a few months later.

Finger movements start at two to four months, when she also begins to make cooing noises. She will refine these skills over the next months.

The pincer grip gives a firm, stable hold on an object, such as a toy brick, so the baby is unlikely to drop it.

Give and take
Grasping and handling objects

1 **I'd like that ball** The baby grasps the ball in a wide power grip, using her whole hand, precisely positioned.

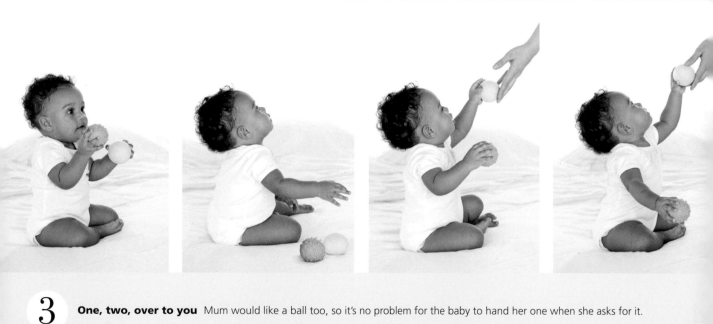

3 **One, two, over to you** Mum would like a ball too, so it's no problem for the baby to hand her one when she asks for it.

From about nine months or so, babies have good hand control and enjoy "give and take" games with other people. They even know how to cope when they're given too many toys to handle at once.

2 **Here comes another one** She can use both hands equally well, and puts down the first ball to take a closer look at the second.

4 **Keep them coming** It's hard to resist a spotty ball, but it's best to put the other toys down first and then examine the collection.

Baby scientist

Babies are natural scientists, and budding mathematicians. They are engaged in constant discovery about how the world around them works.

ONE OF THE MOST fascinating things about babies is how quickly they learn: not even the most powerful computer comes close to the capacity that babies have to absorb and evaluate information. One reason why babies are such good learners is that they function like little scientists, looking for meaningful patterns, coming up with theories about how they think the world works, and looking for evidence that either confirms or dismisses these theories.

> *The human mind is built to find reasons for why things happen… babies put themselves in the best position to find out what these reasons are.*

PHYSICISTS IN TRAINING

Although they probably don't understand why, young babies like to look at things that show cause and effect, such as seeing something move as a result of being bumped or pushed. The human mind is built to find reasons for why things happen, and by watching cause and effect in action, young babies put themselves in the best position to find out what these reasons are.

As babies grow, they start to realize that they, too, can make things happen, for example, pressing a button on a toy to make it light up or move. And just like scientists, babies also carry out experiments. Parents often become exasperated if their baby constantly drops her cup over the edge of the high chair, while watching mum for her reaction. This is how babies experiment: they don't understand about gravity, but they notice that objects can fall. Eventually they accumulate enough evidence to realize that they don't need to do it anymore!

Infant experiments
Babies often experiment by repeatedly dropping a cup onto the floor. Once they are satisfied that cause and effect are shown, they don't feel the need to continue doing it.

{ *They know that objects don't speed up, slow down, or start moving by themselves.* }

EARLY INTUITIONS

Long before babies can properly interact with objects in their world, they already share some of our adult knowledge about how the world works.

Experiments by two developmental psychologists, Elizabeth Spelke and Renee Baillargeon, have shown that young infants have a whole host of expectations about how objects should behave. They know that things don't speed up, slow down, or start moving by themselves. They know that objects don't disappear just because they can't see them anymore. They are also puzzled by events that seem to contradict the laws of nature or their own experience, such as during one experiment when they were shown a video of a toy car seeming to pass through a solid wall.

Babies share our adult intuition that things that move or change their direction by themselves are "alive", like animals. In many cases, this common-sense understanding of the world has ancient origins and is found in our primate ancestors, too.

SPOTTING THE PATTERN

Just as meteorologists look at patterns in data to predict when a hurricane might occur, babies look at patterns to make sense of their world. What babies need to figure out is other people, and this is where their abilities as intuitive statisticians are useful. From early on, babies are sensitive to patterns in human behaviour: they notice that their crying brings mum closer to them, and that when they smile or coo, she'll respond in the same way. As the developmental psychologist Alison Gopnik says, such correspondences are the "statistics of human love".

Baby maths

DISCOVERING THE SCIENCE

SURPRISINGLY, NEWBORN BABIES also have the rudiments of arithmetic. Not only are they able to count small numbers of things, they can even correlate images showing a specific number of objects with the same number represented by beeps or tones. This early recognition that number is an abstract concept is crucial for later mathematical development.

1

Time for mental arithmetic
In this experiment the baby is shown two boxes. She notes that they are completely empty.

One too many biscuits?
Researchers have discovered that babies can't keep track of more than three objects at once, as demonstrated in the biscuit experiment (see right). While Melisa can understand that three biscuits is better than just one, offered the choice of four biscuits or just one, she can't remember which is best.

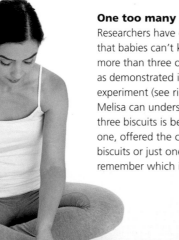

Why can't she remember?
Babies use their short-term memory to keep track of the biscuits in each box – and adding a fourth biscuit seems to break down what's already been stored in the memory.

4

Open the box!
When offered a biscuit, the baby reaches immediate for the second box. She's remembered that there are more biscuits in that box.

{ *... not even the most powerful computer comes close to the capacity that babies have to absorb information.* }

2

Here's one biscuit

One of the boxes is opened, and she sees mum putting one biscuit into the box. The lid is then removed from the second box.

3

And another three biscuits

Three biscuits are placed one by one into the second box. The lids are replaced on both boxes so all biscuits are hidden from the baby's view.

5

Not again!

Now the whole experiment is repeated. This time the baby watches her mum put one biscuit into box one, and four biscuits into the second box.

6

Too much information?

Although the baby has seen the fourth biscuit being put in the second box, she is just as likely to choose the box containing only one biscuit!

The learning brain

A baby learns more quickly during her first years than at any other time in her life, and this amazing capacity for learning is rooted in the brain's remarkable capacity for change.

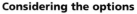

Considering the options
Faced with a problem, babies try to solve it with a whole range of solutions. Figuring out the right one requires a lot of trial and error, but success motivates them to explore and find out more about the world around them.

DURING THE FIRST YEAR of life, the brain continues to grow at its prenatal pace, increasing from 25 per cent to 60 per cent of its adult size. This growth is fuelled by a massive increase in both grey matter (mainly brain cell bodies and the short, tree-like connections between them), and white matter (the long, cable-like axons that reach between the cell bodies). These changes help the baby to learn, and also result from the immense amount of learning that a baby does as she grows.

THE MYELIN EFFECT

After birth (and a little bit beforehand), the brain cell axons start to become coated in a fatty substance called myelin. This process greatly increases the speed and efficiency at which information can travel from cell to cell. It is at its most rapid in the first two years of life, but continues well into adulthood.

Scientists recently discovered that the vocabulary spurt that babies go through at around 18 months seems to follow a period of intense myelination in the language areas of the brain. It might be that only when these areas are sufficiently myelinated are children really able to get to grips with learning words.

VOCABULARY SPURT

Children go from knowing around **50** WORDS at AGE 1 to approximately **5,000** by AGE 6.

In the first year of life the brain continues to grow at its prenatal pace increasing from **25% to 60%** *of its adult size.*

DON'T IGNORE ME!

A baby's brain expects social interaction, love, and being talked to. As long as it gets these things, it will develop normally. But if babies grow up without these basic needs being met, it affects their brain development. Not only are their brains smaller overall, due to less grey and white matter, but they are also less active, like a dimmed light bulb. These effects show how important a baby's early experiences are for brain development.

CREATIVE SOLUTIONS

Babies have an immature frontal cortex, which may in fact be better for creativity. One of the functions of a mature frontal cortex seems to be to limit the options that we consider when problem solving. Neuroscientist Sharon Thompson-Schill believes that when babies face problems, they consider many more options for solving them than adults or older children do. This willingness to consider a whole array of potential solutions (however inappropriate) is key to a creative mind.

DON'T WAKE ME, I'M LEARNING

As well as giving babies the energy they need to explore and play, sleep also seems to play an important role in learning, helping babies to consolidate all their new experiences and transform them into long-term knowledge. Scientists have shown this in a study where babies heard sequences of made-up words, with the same two invented words at the start and end of each sequence. Some babies then took a nap, while others didn't. Afterwards, only the babies who had taken a nap seemed to remember this pattern – and they were even able to remember it 24 hours later.

Brain nurture

With all the classes and products marketed at parents that promise to boost their babies' brains, do any of them stand up to scrutiny?

FOR MOST CHILDREN growing up in loving homes, their parents will provide all they need for healthy brain development without even knowing it. Nevertheless, parents often wonder whether they should be doing anything extra to stimulate their baby's brain and help forge those important connections. They could probably fill their entire week with classes aimed at boosting their child's brainpower – but what does the science say about the impact of all these efforts?

BABY BACH

A popular view is that exposing babies to classical music, even in the womb, will enhance their brain development and intelligence. While there isn't really any scientific evidence to support this idea, scientists have found that babies who join in active music classes for six months show benefits that are not seen in babies who just listen to music passively, including enhanced sensitivity to keys used in Western music, earlier use of communicative gestures, and better social skills.

HAND SIGNALS

Signing common words like "milk" or "more" with babies has become popular, in part due to promises that this will enhance their language development. Although scientific studies have not shown any such benefit,

> { ... parents wonder what to do to stimulate baby and forge important connections. }

parents who sign with their babies do interact differently with them. Not only do they encourage their babies to be more independent and explore more, they also seem to be more tuned in to their babies' communication. While it might not get language off the ground any earlier, baby signing perhaps gives parents an earlier glimpse of an independent mind inside their baby.

COMPUTER BABY

With the advent of tablet computers and smartphones, there is now a whole generation of babies who can swipe their fingers across a screen, and navigate it with impressive precision. To complement these cyber skills, there are now countless "educational" apps aimed at babies and toddlers. So, can we nurture brain and cognitive development with computers? The truth is that we just don't know – there's no data showing that these programs stimulate babies' minds, and the technology is far too recent to know whether there are any long-term costs or benefits. Health experts advise that screen time should be avoided for children under two, in part because time spent in front of a screen is time spent not interacting and talking with adults and other children. But when programs are interactive, the story could be different, although many professionals caution that apps should not be a substitute for real-world exploring.

Exposing your baby to **new experiences** helps her make **new connections** and **pathways** in the brain.

Mime artistes Signing helps some parents feel more in touch at an early stage with what their baby wants to tell them.

Screen genies Children pick up modern technology amazingly quickly. The educational value of apps is debatable, and while they can provide a welcome distraction, there's no substitute for real-life exploration and interaction.

All together now
Actively playing instruments together in groups helps babies to develop more skills than by simply listening to music.

Playing with bubbles

Babies are always entranced by bubbles, as they break all of the physical laws that babies are sensitive to. Yet these simple playthings open a whole world of learning experiences.

Bubbling up Babies can learn a lot from bubbles. They provide a fun way to work on visual tracking, hand-eye coordination, and fine motor skills, such as pointing and using the hands to pop the bubbles. Social and communication skills also come into play – asking for more bubbles and learning to make popping noises.

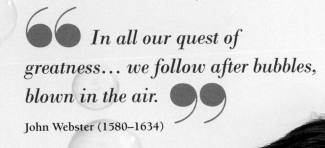

In all our quest of greatness… we follow after bubbles, blown in the air.

John Webster (1580–1634)

Look and learn

No wonder babies spend much of their time intently watching what we are doing. Right from the start, they seem to know that they don't have to discover everything for themselves.

THERE IS LITTLE POINT in reinventing the wheel when you can simply watch how others do things. Fortunately, babies have parents, and perhaps older siblings, who they can watch and copy. Whether this is about how things work or what to do, watching others is a baby's fastest and most efficient way to acquire knowledge.

MINI MIMICS

Everyone finds it amusing when a baby picks up the remote control and points it at the television or puts a phone to her ear. However, this behaviour tells us something very profound about babies: that they are watching what we do, and assuming that our actions have something to teach them. Babies have no idea why pointing the remote control at the television turns it on, but they have realized that the two events are related. Human culture is characterized by tools; things that we have made for a particular purpose. By paying attention to how people around them use tools, babies start to become active participants in their culture.

BROTHERS AND SISTERS

Babies are always interested in what their older siblings are doing, and this is especially true if there is a wide age gap between them. Older children tend to be more focused in their activities and play, which makes it easier for babies to follow what they are doing. They also act like teachers, adjusting their way of doing something or explaining in a simple way so that it is clearer for their young audience. Interestingly, babies who have older siblings seem to do more imitating than babies without any siblings, and will imitate unrelated children, too.

IS IT SAFE?

Babies don't just need to know how something should be done, but also what they should not do. Towards the end of their first year, babies start to look towards their parents for reassurance when they are unsure about something. This could be anything – a new toy, a stranger, or somewhere new that the baby wants to go. They look to their parents to gauge how they should behave, and change their behaviour according to their parents' reaction.

Interestingly, parents' voices seem to be a more powerful source of information for babies than their facial expressions. Babies are more likely to stop doing something if the parent has a worried tone of voice than a worried facial expression. This may be because parents spend a lot of time talking to babies from above or behind while holding them.

LEARNING SPURT
The hippocampus, the area of the brain responsible for memory, is **40**% developed at birth and is fully developed by **18** MONTHS.

CENTRE OF ATTENTION
Parents are under observation from the moment their child first opens her eyes. As the baby grows, mum, dad, and other members of the family become role models for everything she needs to learn to do for herself.

I can do that! Young children catch on quickly to actions they see repeated around them every day. Even technology seems to be no problem – they can often operate the television and DVD player more easily than some adults!

Pass me a brick Babies only occasionally interact with children their own age. They are more inspired by older children, which may encourage them to experiment during play.

Babies are less likely to copy someone who speaks a foreign language, rather than their own.

Let me show you Older children make great teachers. Babies are more interested in what a slightly older child is doing than a teenager or an adult, because they can relate their own level of skill much better to a child that is not too far ahead of them developmentally. An older child is also much less likely to give the baby more help and advice than she wants than a parent.

Not so sure As babies become more adventurous, they begin to use their parents' reactions as a guide to what's safe. If picked up by a stranger, they may look back at mum for reassurance and affirmation of how they should react. Similarly, they may wait to see mum's expression before touching a new toy or rushing off to explore an unfamiliar place.

On reflection

Mirrors and reflections fascinate young babies, yet the journey to self-recognition is a slow one.

BABY FACTS

MIRROR RECOGNITION

Hold a mirror in front of a seven-month-old and she'll happily try to engage the new "playmate", unaware of who it is. As she gets older, she'll begin to notice that when she moves her hand, for example, the hand in the mirror moves too – and eventually she'll realize that she's actually looking at herself.

Red spot test, stage one Seven-month-old Melisa is fascinated by the baby in the mirror, but doesn't know that it is her own image she can see, or that the spot is on her own cheek.

Red spot test, stage two Four-year-old Helin is fully aware of what she sees in the mirror, and knows that the red spot she can see means there's a spot on her own face.

IT'S NOT UNTIL babies are around 18 months old that most begin to recognize themselves in a mirror or a photograph. Psychologists think this is because a baby needs to reach the stage where she realizes that she is an individual, just like other people, before she can comprehend that the baby in the mirror is herself.

One way that researchers have investigated this kind of awareness is the red spot test. If you secretly put a red spot on an older child's face and ask her to look in the mirror, she'll put her hand to the spot and wonder how it got there. A few other species, such as chimpanzees and orangutans, also do this – but a young human baby doesn't. Even though she sees the spot on the baby in the mirror, she doesn't realize it's on her own face.

As she matures, as well as making the connection between what she sees in the mirror and herself, a baby also begins to show her self-awareness in other ways, such as using words to refer to herself.

Mirror mirror on the wall Although at seven months she is unable to recognize herself, Melisa can recognize her sister perfectly, and looks at her image with great interest.

Communication

Joining in

Right from the start, babies are social creatures – and they learn how to work this to their advantage. At this young age, babies rely on parents and carers for their route to a social world.

AS HUMANS, babies will grow up to be members of the most cooperative species on Earth. This instinctive desire to cooperate and engage with others is evident even in newborns, and develops throughout childhood.

PLAY WITH ME!

A newborn already commands the attention of others, and soon learns that she also has the power to influence what they do. If a baby stops sucking during a feed, it provokes the adult to interact with her – jiggling, stroking, talking to her, and gazing into her eyes. The baby notices this, and so she does it again and again.

Babies soon begin to notice other times when they can reliably get a response. When babies make cooing noises, adults copy them; and when they smile, adults always smile back. This interaction is so important to babies that they become quite upset if people don't respond to their bids for communication. If a mum just looks at her two-month-old baby with a completely still, expressionless face, the baby will become upset, as if she can't understand why her mother won't talk to her.

As babies get older, this expectation that people will engage with them extends to other behaviours. For instance, in a turn-taking game, such as passing a ball back and forth, if the adult stops playing, the baby will try various ways to get the adult to start playing again.

CATCHING THE EYE

Eye contact is so important for our social interactions that scientists think humans evolved unique eyes just for this purpose. Humans are the only species that have white eyeballs, which makes it easy to see if someone is looking at you, and in which direction the iris and pupil are moving. In most other animals the eyeball (sclera), is

0–2years
At this age, babies will play happily alongside each other ("parallel play") but won't actively play together. They return the friendship of others, especially that of older children, but do not make friends for themselves.

2–3years
As toddlers they slowly begin to learn the skill of making friends. However, at this stage they are likely to be more attracted by the actual game someone else is playing, rather than by a particular child.

3+years
At this age, older toddlers begin to select their activities in order to be with a particular child. And, although they make real friendships, they still may not be fully willing to share possessions.

brown, and for many species eye contact is actually a sign of aggression. But for us, cooperating with each other is such an important feature of our way of life that our eyes evolved not just for seeing, but as a means of getting others' attention and communicating with them.

NOT FAIR!

Babies' innate sociability may explain why they have a sense of how we should behave towards each other. Even by three months, babies prefer to interact with people they have seen behaving nicely towards others, rather than unkindly. And by eight months, they seem to share our adult opinion that crime deserves punishment. Our sense of justice may have evolved to protect us from those who don't play nicely, so even babies understand that we should help, not hinder, each other.

Parallel play Up to about the age of two, babies engage primarily in "parallel play", where they play by themselves, but alongside another child.

BABY FACTS

Babies are built to enjoy interacting with other people. They love making eye contact and naturally join in with turn-taking games.

Making faces

A baby will use facial expressions to try to tell people around her how she is feeling. Until she is able to speak, making faces or crying are her main means of communication.

THE EXPRESSION ON A BABY'S FACE is a good indicator of what she is thinking and feeling. It's her way of saying: "It feels good, keep going" or "This isn't very nice at all"! As babies grow and start to acquire a better understanding of the world, and better control of their facial muscles, basic expressions of like or dislike are replaced by more complex looks that demonstrate surprise, sadness, anger, and fear.

SHOWING EMOTION

We all use similar facial expressions to show emotions, such as joy, anger, fear, and disgust; these are crucial if they are to be understood by others. Indeed, it is believed (and Darwin was the first to suggest it) that facial expressions have evolved to allow humans to communicate real or imagined states – so that others will react appropriately. Disgust, expressed when eating something, would make other people avoid a potentially dangerous food. Other researchers have suggested that facial expressions are merely a result of an individual's physiological reaction to their environment. For example, if someone is scared, they breathe heavily and their blood flow increases in preparation for fight or flight. Wide open eyes and a fearful expression allow the person to take in more of their visual field, and be more likely to see anything suspicious happening. However, it is the role facial

> During the first weeks, babies smile more often while sleeping than they do when awake.

expressions have to play in communication and social interaction that makes them so important. There is no better example to illustrate this than smiling, which starts very early on in life.

NEWBORN SMILING

Seeing a newborn baby smile while asleep is possibly one of the most beautiful, yet puzzling, behaviours. During the first weeks of life, babies smile more often while sleeping than they do when awake. Premature infants smile even more, and prenatal scans have also shown babies smiling in the womb. Although infants do appear to dream, at this early stage of life it is unlikely that babies smile because of their dreams. Researchers believe that prenatal and newborn smiling serves two functions. First, it is a way of rehearsing an important method of communication that infants will use later. Second, it has an immediate effect on those around them, who may not otherwise be inclined to carry on feeding, cuddling, and nappy changing.

As babies start to smile more at people during the day, sleep smiles cease to be useful, and gradually vanish. However, premature infants continue smiling in their sleep for longer than full-term babies, suggesting that a biological clock encoded in the genes is responsible for this behaviour.

WHY INFANTS SMILE

Babies seem to smile randomly in the first few weeks, and any attempts to make them smile will often fail. Around two months of age, infants start smiling more during social interactions than when they are alone. Seeing a face and hearing a voice are the most effective ways of making a baby smile. At this age, it is her mother's face that triggers the most smiles – the baby's eyes are now capable of focusing on facial features, and she starts to recognize familiar faces.

IN THE GENES

Babies don't need to see other people smile to do it, too. Blind babies smile in response to a familiar voice, and all babies smile before birth. The facial expressions of babies born blind are similar to those of their relatives, indicating that genes play a role in the facial movements used to express emotions. However, the smiles of blind infants are less frequent and more fleeting than those of sighted infants, which means that reciprocation is vital in maintaining this expression.

THE HAPPY SMILE

In the first year, it is interaction with people, and taking turns smiling and vocalizing that keeps baby and mother happy. Just like adults, babies smile in different ways. When genuinely happy, adults slightly close the eyes, and open the mouth. One hypothesis is that eye constriction reduces the visual field, so that the focus is on the object of the emotion, and distractions are filtered out. Although younger babies produce this smile indiscriminately, by 10 months they are more likely to do this when approached by their smiling mothers, but smile without eye constriction if approached by an impassive stranger.

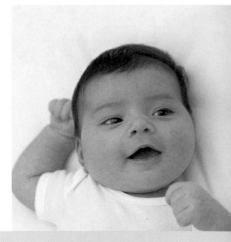

All is well in my world

NEGATIVE EXPRESSIONS

Unlike smiling, negative expressions are not consistent. For example, 10- to 12-month-olds might show surprise and fear when faced with a sudden drop in height, yet at other times, the infant may look as if in pain. Sour tastes make some babies look disgusted; others look sad. When crying, they might display frustration, fear, and sadness. The variability may be because young infants don't yet know why they feel discomfort, and what should be done about it. An expression of distress will succeed in making adults try to identify the cause, and remove it promptly.

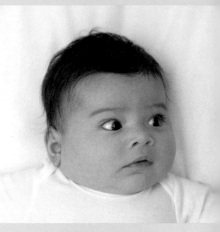

That's a surprise!

YUM OR YUCK

Food can trigger different expressions. If given something sweet, newborns will raise the corners of their mouth as if smiling, and stick their tongues out to lick their lips. If they are given something bitter, they will open the mouth wide, probably to remove the unpleasant taste, squint their eyes, and wrinkle their noses. The reason for these "disgust" expressions being present so early on – when a baby's diet consists of nothing but milk – may be that they protect babies from being given the wrong food by their siblings, who sometimes play at feeding the baby.

I can't decide if I like that.

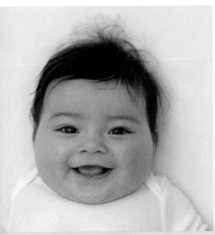

I'm feeling quite happy.

Hello, Mummy, it's lovely to see you!

You're a stranger, but you look nice.

I'm not very happy at the moment.

That really is not nice!

That's horrible, I don't want any more!

Not too sure about this.

I definitely don't like it.

Great, give me some more!

Let's play!

At around six months, babies start gurgling and laughing at the world around them – and in particular at the people around them. How, and why, do they start enjoying the world and the games they play with others?

BABY FACTS

Neuropsychologists think that the sound of infant laughter prompts the release of hormones that may activate reward centres in the parent's brain.

Repetitive play is highly important in developing a baby's social and turn-taking skills.

adult gives baby attention • baby laughs • laughter gets attention • adult repeats •

Babies anticipate what's going to happen by remembering patterns of sound and movement by the parent.

VERY SMALL BABIES don't really play with other babies. Play is something that develops as they become toddlers, even though toddlers stick mainly with "parallel play", doing things alongside each other rather than sharing games. However, play still has a very important role in babies' social development, because it is one of the crucial ways in which they engage with adults and start to interact and communicate with them in a way that goes beyond their immediate needs.

Laughter, for small babies, is a crucial part of this – it is one of the first structured sounds they learn to produce, and it instantly prompts an adult response. They don't necessarily laugh at a "joke" as adults understand it, but as part of a social exchange. The games that adults play with babies to make them laugh are social interactions in the style of conversations – but long before the baby has any concept of speech.

THE ELEMENT OF SURPRISE

The key theme of almost all adult-and-baby games – giving and taking away, hiding and showing, and chasing games – is a sequence: something is about to happen; there is a period of watching and waiting; the action happens; and then there is a response. Whatever form the action takes, it depends on very close attention, watching the other person, and learning the "cues" on both sides.

In the very early days, these games are entirely initiated by the adult. As babies grow up, they start taking the lead in initiating the conversation, to the point where they take over. They also begin to find things "funny" – or more accurately, surprising or incongruous – and laugh at that, because they have learned how to make sense of a small part of the world. Once they have an idea of what should happen, they burst out laughing if the expected pattern is disrupted.

On top of that, play is simply – and importantly – enjoyable on its own. Play helps children to make sense of the world around them and furthers their emotional development. This is why "play therapy" is such a valuable part of treating troubled children – but it is also fun for its own sake. Play is widely acknowledged to be an essential part of children's development and their social wellbeing, from babyhood onwards.

Laughter and giggles

Laughing is one of our human instincts, and it forms part of a baby's emerging need to socialize and bond with others. It also has roots deep in our evolutionary history.

ANCIENT LAUGHTER

Researchers have analysed the laughter patterns of humans and great apes, concluding that laughter may date back at least 10–15 million years, to the last common ancestor of modern great apes and humans. They think that humans developed our distinctive laugh after we separated from the ancestors we share with bonobos and chimps – about 4.5 to 6 million years ago.

 *Laughter is one of the things you can share when you meet someone, even if you don't share the same culture. Laughter has a way of being inclusive. That applies to babies, even more, because they're completely non-threatening.*

Dr Caspar Addyman,
Babylab at Birkbeck

Peekaboo!
Baby's favourite game?

DISCOVERING THE SCIENCE

1 **Surprise appearance** For babies younger than about six to eight months, the charm of peekaboo is the surprise of someone popping up, as if for the first time – because they don't know that people and things carry on existing, even if they can't be seen.

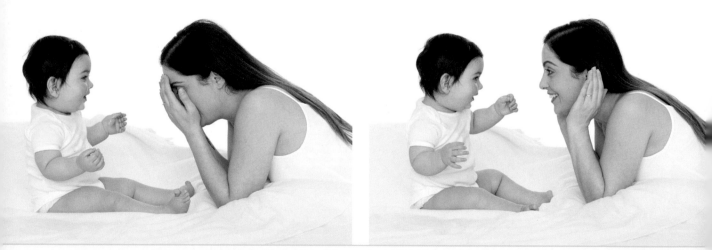

2 **Here's looking at you** Older babies aren't so shocked by the peekaboo disappearing trick – instead, they're waiting in delicious anticipation for the other person to reappear. At around a year, babies start to realize that they have the power to

Why is peekaboo babies' favourite game?
The answer demonstrates how babies' sense of fun and humour develops month by month.

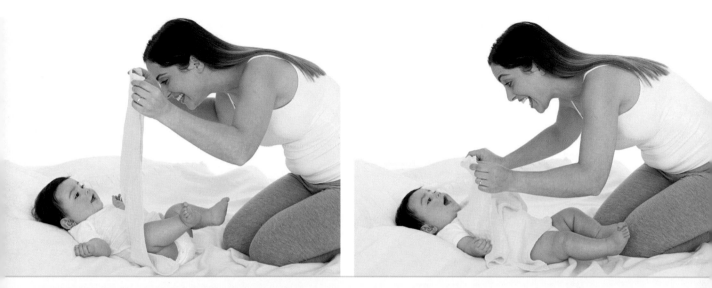

But babies of all ages enjoy the fun and expectation involved in playing a favourite game with someone familiar. Even if the trick is always the same, it still gets a laugh from both players.

make adults laugh, and then the games become much more of a two-way tease. And by 18 months, babies are often playing peekaboo to get a good reaction from the adult, rather than the other way around.

What's that?

Long before they can talk, babies have clever ways of gathering information and learning words. Central to this is the ability to identify what others are indicating, and to indicate things themselves.

AS BABIES BEGIN to show an interest in things around them, parents nurture this curiosity by teaching them words – often by pointing or gazing at something and telling the baby what it's called. At the heart of this is "joint attention", where baby and parent look at something together, sharing their interest and excitement.

But how do babies understand that when an adult points to something, they are not trying to draw the baby's attention to their finger, but to the ball over there on the grass? It's not a trivial task, but by the time they reach their first birthday, and often before, babies do understand this – and start pointing by themselves.

Babies vary in their **gaze-following skills,** and scientists have shown that a baby's ability to follow someone's gaze at **10 months** is directly related to **their language skills at 18 months.**

POINT IT OUT

Babies begin to follow pointing accurately at around 10 months. Scientists think that if babies sense that someone is making a communicative gesture, such as pointing, they automatically pay attention to what the person is trying to teach them about. So, if a baby sees someone pointing to a bicycle, they will pay special attention to what the bicycle looks like, and remember its two wheels and handlebars – rather than, say, its location. By remembering its appearance the baby can then recognize other objects that are also bicycles, and extend the correct word to these similar things.

LOOK THIS WAY

It's not until around six months that a baby begins to routinely look in the direction towards which someone else is looking. Initially, they will follow an adult's gaze only if eye contact is first established: babies seem to interpret this as a sign that they should pay attention. Later on, they will check someone's gaze direction before learning a new word: if a baby hears the word "aeroplane" while playing with a toy car, she won't assume that the toy car is called an aeroplane, instead she will check to see what the person is looking at.

I CAN POINT TOO!

At around 12 months, most babies will start to point themselves. To begin with, they point to try to get things they want, but soon it becomes a way to share their interests. When babies point, parents usually say the name of the object the baby is indicating. Pointing then becomes a useful way in which babies can request information about things they are interested in. How much a baby points relates to language development later on, probably because those who point more provide themselves with more opportunities for learning words.

FOLLOWING A GAZE

Gaze-following is an important way in which babies start to understand what someone is trying to tell them. While newborns show a rudimentary form of this, by six months a baby's gaze-following skills are more adept.

1

Establishing eye contact
To begin with, an adult needs to establish eye contact with the baby, so that they are holding each other's attention.

2

Looking towards object
Once Mum has got her baby's attention, she turns her head and eyes towards a nearby object – the teddy bear.

3

Following the gaze
The baby turns her own gaze to follow her mother's. They are now focused on the same thing and Mum can tell her about it. Bingo!

Look this way
I can point too!

1 **Getting her attention** Mum points something out with her finger, and Melisa turns to look.

2 **Holding her attention** But keeping her focused on the object is tricky – Melisa is more interested in mum!

4 **Concentrating properly** She sees the object again and focuses her attention on it.

5 **Reaching out** Slowly she extends her hand to copy her mother's while continuing to look at the object.

After mastering gaze-following, babies develop the ability to follow pointing – and once they master the art of pointing themselves, a whole new world of learning opens up.

POKING OR POINTING

Index finger pointing may have its origins in our pincer grip. After mastering the pincer grip, babies may start investigating things around them by poking them with their index finger and, later, this poking might evolve into pointing. Some babies begin pointing with their index fingers, others with their whole hands.

3 **Following a direction** Back to the task in hand, Melisa is again shown where the object is.

LEARNING IN THE DARK

Gaze-following and pointing are useful ways for babies to learn words, yet they are not essential. Blind children cannot follow a gaze or pointing, and do not develop pointing themselves. Nevertheless, they do not appear to be particularly delayed in their language development. Instead of using pointing to gather information, they rely more on speech to learn words.

6 **Finally getting the point** That's it! At last Melisa gets the message and is pointing on her own.

Who's that beautiful baby?

Qui est ce beau bébé?

Wer ist das schöne Baby?

Kuka on tuo kaunis vauva?

¿Quién es ese hermoso bebé?

Chi è quel bel bambino?

I can learn any language on Earth!

Multilingual baby: The sounds a baby makes are universal, and a baby can listen to and learn any language as a tiny tot. It is only as babies get older that they start to sound different according to their native language.

First sounds

Learning to talk is a complicated business: the mouth, throat, brain, and ears are all involved. It's no surprise, then, that it takes babies a while to coordinate everything before starting to speak.

FROM THE MOMENT they first draw breath, babies are capable of making a great deal of noise. As well as producing volume they can also imitate voices they hear, but can't do this with any precision until they are a few months old. From about six weeks they start making vowel sounds (the cooing or wailing of "aaa-aaa" and "ooo-ooo"), using the back of the vocal tract with a closed throat and little breath support. Even at this early stage, babies mimic the speech patterns and language that they hear by making inarticulate sounds in the same pattern. Sound is produced when the vocal folds (once called the vocal cords) vibrate in the larynx (voice box) at the top of the neck. Air pushes through the larynx and up through the throat, mouth, and nose to produce what we think of as "voice".

LEARNING TO BABBLE

At the age of two or three months, babies start to laugh. As they reach six months they gain more control over their voice and can open their throats and push breath through in vocal play, putting consonants and vowels together, growling, squealing, and blowing raspberries. Speech is still some way off, but they're starting to articulate sounds like "ba" and "da". Also at around six months they begin to babble, repeating a syllable such as "dadada" before moving on to sequences that sound like words, but aren't.

So how do babies start to produce language? Those first noises build into words by intensive training. There's evidence that babies have an innate skill for developing language that is activated by hearing people speak and repeat sounds back to them. In fact, researchers have found that even deaf babies will initially babble aloud, but the lack of new sound inputs for them to hear and repeat inhibits their progress. Gradually, babies' perception and babbling tunes in to the language they hear most often: for example, a French baby will babble very differently from a Japanese baby.

VOICE CONTROL

Babies younger than four or five months old can't make proper speech-like sounds for anatomical reasons: the voice box is high in the throat, so that the baby can breathe and drink while breastfeeding. In fact, the cries of young infants are more like the distress calls of primates than later speech sounds. But, by five months, the voice box has dropped, the baby's control of her vocal muscles has developed, and she can make deliberate noises.

… The sounds a baby makes are universal, and a baby can listen to and learn any language as a tiny tot…

Getting the meaning

Babies begin to understand the meanings of words several months before they start using them, and the special way that their parents talk to them helps them to learn.

THE FIRST STAGE of learning to talk is listening. The sense of hearing develops in the womb, so babies are used to hearing voices well before they are born. From birth, babies enjoy being talked to – even when they have no clue what is being said – and by listening to the sounds going on around them, they can begin to interpret what it all means.

WORD RECOGNITION

Many babies start to say a few recognizable words from around the age of 10 months, but their actual understanding of some words starts well before this. It's been shown that babies as young as six months can recognize some familiar words, such as "nose" or "banana". So before they are even crawling, they have already picked out these sounds from the jumble of speech they hear around them, connected them to objects they have seen, and remembered the connection.

BABY TALK

Parents can help babies master the meaning of words by using "baby talk" – a simplified, emphatic way of talking with a higher pitch than normal adult speech. This helps it stand out from general background noise and attracts the baby's attention.

When speaking in baby talk, parents use a number of ways to get the meaning across to their child. They speak more slowly, use shorter sentences, and talk about things the baby can see ("Look! A train!"). Sounds are exaggerated for emphasis, or repeated ("woof-woof") and marked by a rising pitch at the end of a sentence.

Researchers from two US universities have shown that baby talk can have great benefits – particularly when it comes from an adult talking to just one child. The more that parents exaggerated their vowels and raised the pitch of their voices, the more their babies babbled back, and more words they mastered.

THINKING AHEAD

Babies learn action words better before the action has happened. The word "open" is more likely to be learnt after hearing "Shall we open it?" than "It's open". Babies seem to anticipate what's likely to be done, then match the word they hear with the imagined action.

SOUND PATTERNS

At 4½ months babies can recognize the sound patterns of their own name and can distinguish it from other names with the same number of syllables and inflection. Babies learn vowels faster than consonants because these sounds carry better and are easier to make.

BABY FACTS

You don't have to be an adult to talk baby talk. Four-year-old Helin can speak it well with her baby sister, even if Melisa can't understand what she's saying!

First words

By the time they are about a year or so old, many babies are beginning to say their first words – this is the start of their journey to becoming fully fledged experts in their native language.

WHILE MANY PARENTS proudly note down their own baby's first words (beyond mama and dada) as a sign of their emerging personality, in fact babies' first words are usually predictable: names of familiar people, animals, food, vehicles, or toys. Things that move, such as pets or cars, are particularly likely to be the first things that babies talk about. But this is just the beginning, and once a baby has mastered the art of a few words, the flood gates will open and her vocabulary will start to develop more rapidly.

LOST IN TRANSLATION

Of course babies don't get the words exactly right at first, and there can be a lot of confusion and misunderstandings to begin with. It falls to the parents to take on the role of translator for quite some time.

However, it's no surprise that early attempts to pronounce words don't work too well – the muscles in the face, mouth, and tongue have first to develop and then practice is needed to coordinate them.

Common mistakes when trying out words are leaving out the first or final consonants (for example, "nana" for banana, or "ba" for ball); simplifying consonant clusters ("brekwust" for breakfast or "top" for stop); and leaving out or repeating whole syllables ("dadad" for dad).

At the age of 18 months to two years, children often start to use two-word sentences, and may know about 100 WORDS. By the time an infant is three years old she may have a vocabulary of around 3,000 WORDS.

CHATTERBOX

Around 18 months of age, babies' appetite for learning new words increases dramatically. At this age, they are adding to their vocabulary at a very impressive rate – sometimes up to 40 words a week. By this point they have discovered words that describe actions, such as "push" or "see", as well as objects, plus other useful words like "more", "big", "pretty", or "bad".

This is the age when they also discover the real secret of language: that by using several words together, they can say all sorts of new things. Armed with these mental tools, babies can really begin to express themselves, perhaps demanding "more milk", or chastising a naughty toy – "bad teddy".

GETTING THE HANG OF IT

As they build their word knowledge, babies are also picking up the structure of their native language, and by the middle of their third year they begin to use sentences, and even to get the hang of simple grammar – for example, in the English language, adding an "s" to words to form plurals. But other elements of grammatical speech take longer to grasp: by the time children start school, they will still be making linguistic mistakes that entertain – or frustrate – their parents.

Things that move, such as pets or cars, are … likely to be the first things that babies talk about.

Mama!

Hello, darling!

Forming the words

ONCE A BABY has managed to coordinate the many vocal and facial muscles that are needed for speech, she will be eager to communicate with those around her. A study in 2012 revealed that babies first learn language by watching the shapes that their mum's lips make.

WORKING OUT WHAT'S WHAT

Babies have to work out what words mean, and part of this is deciding whether, for example, the word "daddy" refers to just one person, or to everyone who looks a bit like him (all men, perhaps).
Babies and children naturally generalize from knowing a word that applies to one thing, to guessing what else it applies to – with intriguing results.
Here are some real examples:

BALL: anything round, for example, apples, eggs, light spot from a torch
HORSE, COWS, PIGS: any four-legged animals
SCISSORS: all metal objects
FLY: insects, specks of dirt, toes
LABEL: unwanted, string-like things, such as orange pith and tiny fishbones

WORD SKILLS

Researchers have noticed that the type of words that babies say early on is associated with their later progress in mastering language. "Referential" babies, who use a lot of object words, tend to be good at gaining a good vocabulary fast; while "reflective" babies, who prefer to talk about people, are quicker to get to grips with grammar and to move on to more complex speech.

FROM SOUNDS TO SPEECH

0–6
WEEKS
Crying, burps, sucking

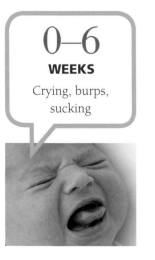

6–10
WEEKS
Cooing, laughing

4–6
MONTHS
Vocal play

6–12
MONTHS
Babbling

BABY FACTS

The best way for parents to help a baby to learn new words is by saying the word she is aiming for – rather than simply mimicking what she says, if she has made a mistake.

CLUCKS AND PURRS

Animal noises are often some of the first recognizable "words" that babies say – but these vary across languages (or so the speakers believe). A cat purrs "goro goro" in Japanese, "ronron" in French, and "doromb" in Hungarian. Turkish hens cluck "gut gut gdak" and Dutch ones "tok tok". Dog barks vary from "vov-vov" in Danish to "bau-bau" in Italian. But donkey brays – apparently – sound pretty much the same in most countries around the world!

12–18
MONTHS
Single words

18–24
MONTHS
Two-word speech

2–2½
YEARS
Multi-word speech

2½
YEARS ONWARDS
Full sentences

Double talk

Young children's brains are so absorbent that they can pick up two (or more) languages at once. An extra language provides a potentially lifelong skill, and may enhance a child's mental abilities, too.

SOME CHILDREN LEARN more than one language in their early years. This may happen when a child learns one language from parents at home and a second at school, or if the parents are of different nationalities and use both languages at home from birth.

In the early 20th century, language experts claimed that bilingualism confused children and delayed mental development. However, these ideas were based on studies that didn't take into account external factors, such as social background. More recent studies have revealed that bilingual children not only acquire language almost as quickly as monolingual children, but may gain significant mental benefits, too.

> Bilingualism may help to delay the onset of Alzheimer's disease – a common form of dementia.

GOOD FOR THE BRAIN

Bilingualism is good for brain function, as the brain must constantly evaluate language it hears in order to process it correctly. Studies of bilingual children have shown them to demonstrate increased levels in certain aspects of cognitive performance, such as decision-making. Such tasks require use of the brain's "executive function" – its ability to prioritize complex tasks and switch mental gears. The executive function of bilingual babies appears to be more advanced than that of monolingual babies, perhaps because they make more use of it in order to monitor input from two languages.

But these mental benefits do not stop at childhood. Another study shows that the age of onset of Alzheimer's disease – the most common form of senile dementia – is more than four years later in bilinguals than monolinguals. Scientists suspect this is because bilingualism exercises the brain, building up cognitive reserves that protect against dementia.

Although bilingualism may seem like a fairly effortless path to acquiring languages, there are consequences. One of the main ones is "language attrition" – when a child loses the ability to speak one language if the other becomes too dominant, such as if she starts to favour the language she uses at school and shares with friends. However, she may still understand the other language.

WHO SAYS WHAT

To prevent language attrition, some parents use a strict "one person one language" system, with each parent sticking to their native language. Others opt to use one language at home – typically an immigrant language – and another outside the home. This system has disadvantages, though, as a child may start school with poor language skills. Many parents report that achieving bilingualism gets easier with the second child – the first child is often a natural chatterbox by the time a sibling arrives, and provides endless free language training.

> 66 *To have another language is to possess a second soul.* 99
>
> Emperor Charlemagne (c.747– c.814)

I speak Malay and Indonesian.

I speak French and Berber.

I speak German and Dutch.

THE BEST TIMES FOR LEARNING A SECOND LANGUAGE

In order to become actively bilingual, a child needs to spend one-third of her waking hours exposed to a second language. The younger the child, the better she can absorb language; as she ages, her ability to learn to speak a new language fluently declines.

0–3 YEARS

She is learning her first language and her mind is open and flexible – she can learn multiple languages and will speak them as a native.

4–7 YEARS

At this stage, she is still able to process multiple languages on parallel paths – she doesn't use one language to translate the other.

8–14 YEARS

After puberty, new languages are acquired more slowly, and a child (or adult) may use their native language as a path to the new one.

Becoming an individual

Week one…

MELISA'S FIRST WEEK in the world has been an exciting time for her family. They are getting to know this tiny new addition and are beginning to notice little things about her – the sound of her cry, the way she moves her hands and feet, and when she wants a cuddle from mum. Melisa herself will not remember anything about this time. But while she seems to be occupied solely with eating and sleeping, slowly she is starting to take in all the new things in the world around her.

One year on…

BY THE TIME of her first birthday, Melisa has come on in leaps and bounds and is now a bonny, bouncing baby. She is actively crawling and pulling herself up and will soon be walking. Her first teeth have come through and she is enjoying new foods and tastes. Like all one-year-olds, she is fascinated by everything around her and is eager to find out more. From now on, it's onwards and upwards!

The genetic factor

Every baby has an inbuilt set of genetic instructions for making a new individual. But who this baby will become depends on a complex interaction between the baby's genes and the environment.

CURLED UP IN THE CENTRE of every human body cell are 23 pairs of chromosomes, which hold tens of thousands of genes. Genes, made from DNA, are strung together on these coiled chromosomes to provide a detailed blueprint for making everything in the body.

THE GENETIC CODE

These genetic blueprints code for everything from a baby's sex, eye, and hair colour, to quirkier characteristics, such as the shape of her hairline, or whether her cheeks will crease into dimples when she smiles.

Some characteristics are straightforwardly genetic: blood group, for example. But others, including height, intelligence, personality aspects, and the risk of illnesses, such as heart disease, are only partially heritable. While such traits are underscored by a person's genetics, they are also affected by environmental factors, such as nutrition, socioeconomic status, and family upbringing. Changes in environmental factors can affect whole populations: increasing economic wealth as well as advances in nutrition and healthcare have meant that many countries have seen the average height of their populations rise over the last 50 years.

Since the 1960s
the average height of
11-year-old
Japanese boys has increased
by 5.5 inches.

A baby has roughly half the same genes as her sister… but it's possible that while she's received one piece of a chromosome from her mum, her sister has inherited a different piece of the same chromosome.

Grandmother

Around a quarter of Melisa's genes come from her grandmother. Sometimes characteristics can skip generations, so Melisa may inherit things from her grandmother that don't show in her mother.

Mum

Babies inherit genetic traits, such as medical conditions, from both parents, but scientists are now looking at how the mother's pregnancy – particularly her diet – can affect genes in ways that influence the baby's future health.

Dad

Dad's genes played a key role in deciding Melisa's sex. She has inherited the X chromosome from the XY pairing in his sex chromosomes, which combine with an X from her mother's to make her a girl.

FAMILY INFLUENCES

How tall will Melisa grow? How intelligent will she be? And what kind of person might she be as an adult? These are questions that every family might wonder about a new baby. While only time will tell, looking at the parents may reveal something about that baby's potential.

Although children are half mum and half dad, they may not always resemble their parents, or look like anyone in the wider family either. This is because in every generation, genes are mixed up and shuffled around like a deck of cards – and you never know which genes are going to be donated by each parent. You may inherit some genes in forms that don't play out, so that you do not see their effects: these are "recessive", overruled by any "dominant" versions, and that is why certain recessive characteristics may skip a generation.

Most physical characteristics – including hair, eye, or skin colour – depend on more than just one gene. That's why in families of mixed ethnic heritage, children in the same family may have differently coloured skin or hair: it's because of the complexity of these genes and the interplay of dominant and recessive versions. It's also what makes wondering what a baby will look like so fascinating.

> { *Curled up in the centre of every human body cell are* **23 pairs of chromosomes,** *which hold tens of thousands of genes.* }

INHERITANCE

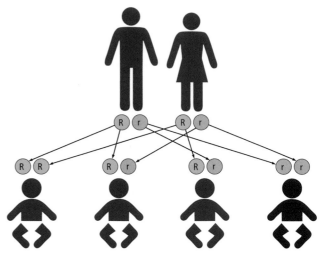

Attached or unattached? Characteristics such as earlobe shape are inherited from a combination of genes from both parents. The parents (above) have unattached earlobes. Each has a dominant gene (R) and a recessive gene (r). Three of their children inherit one dominant gene and have unattached earlobes, the fourth child inherits two recessive genes and consequently, has attached earlobes.

WHO'S THE DADDY?

"Doesn't he look like his father!" may be the reaction of many a relative to a new baby in the family. But do babies look more like their dads than their mums? This would make evolutionary sense, ensuring that dad carries on providing for the child. However, recent studies suggest mums are biased towards saying their newborns look like dad – even when others think they don't!

Nature is all that a man brings with himself into the world; nurture is every influence without that affects him after his birth.

Sir Francis Galton (1822–1911)

Boys and girls

Just six weeks into pregnancy, hormonal changes mean that a fetus will start to develop as either a boy or a girl. But when it comes to growing up, gender differences are not always so clear cut.

AT THE MOST BASIC LEVEL, sex is hardwired into the genes. For the first few weeks of a pregnancy, there is no difference between a male and female embryo. Then at around six weeks, the sex chromosomes the embryo has inherited from its parents "switch on" the hormones that will determine whether the fetus develops into a boy or a girl. And yet, although there are clear physical differences between boys and girls, what actually constitutes gender has long been a hotly debated topic.

WHAT IS GENDER?

Once a baby is born, like it or not, parents and others may assign certain behaviours and characteristics to being a boy, or being a girl. Society has differing expectations of men and women, and some believe that it is these expectations that shape boys and girls into traditional gender roles. Others argue that gender differences are inherent in a child, and that environment has little to do with how they turn out.

Untangling how much of boyish or girly behaviour is down to nature and nurture is tough. It is most likely to be due to a combination of both, though nurture may reinforce certain traits. For example, that girls may grow up to be empathetic and caring may be in part enhanced by the expectation in many cultures that one day they will grow up to be mothers.

> At birth, the male baby brain is 12–20% larger than the female baby brain.

PEER PRESSURE

To an extent, boys will be boys and girls will be girls because they want to conform to their peer group. Some time in their second year, a child becomes aware of his or her own gender identity and that of other people – and being different can be a social taboo.

BRAINS AND ABILITIES

Whether boys' and girls' brains are programmed to develop differently is a matter of debate. What is known is that boys' brains tend to be about 12 to 20 per cent bigger than girls' at birth. Boys are thought to have better spatial abilities compared with girls, but are more vulnerable to developmental problems, such as autism, and also language problems, such as dyslexia.

In terms of education, it's been suggested that girls are better at literacy and boys better at mathematics. Globally, boys do seem to perform better in maths, but a study that compared the test scores of over 275,000 teenagers in 40 countries revealed that this may be due to social influences: the gender gap closes in countries with more egalitarian attitudes towards the sexes.

Baby girls may be more sensitive to touch than boys, and more adept at language – but again, adult treatment may bear an influence: one study suggests that mums talk more to daughters than they do to sons.

GENETIC MIX

At the moment of conception, two sex chromosomes (one from each parent) fuse together as the embyro forms. It is this combination of sex chromosomes – either XX or XY – that determines the baby's sex.

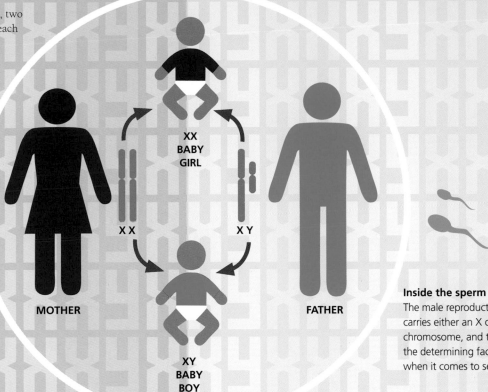

MOTHER

FATHER

XX
BABY
GIRL

X X

X Y

XY
BABY
BOY

Inside the egg
The female reproductive cell carries the X chromosome. At conception, it fuses with a sperm and the chromosomes combine.

Inside the sperm
The male reproductive cell carries either an X or a Y chromosome, and this is the determining factor when it comes to sex.

DEVELOPING FEMALE

It was once thought that females were the "default" sex, because they lack the sudden boost of testosterone that "switches on" male genes at around six weeks of development. However, it is now believed that genetic changes at this time are more complex, and specific female genes also switch on in female embryos.

DEVELOPING MALE

The boost of testosterone that baby boys receive in the womb at around six weeks is what results in the formation of male sex organs. But they continue to produce large amounts of testosterone during their development, so that a baby boy is born with as much testosterone as a 25-year-old man. These levels drop suddenly at birth.

Gendered play

Put any bunch of toddlers in a room of toys, and you are likely to see boys zooming cars around and girls playing with dolls. And everyone knows of a little girl who loves pink, even if her parents have tried their hardest to broaden her colour horizons.

Some scientific studies suggest that these kind of gender preferences may be hardwired to some extent. The gender preference for "masculine" toys, such as cars, has been shown to relate to the boost of testosterone that baby boys are exposed to in the womb – one study linked high-levels of fetal testosterone to typical male-play behaviour in boys later on. Boys are often more active than girls and enjoy wrestling and rolling around, especially with dad. Some scientists believe this play-fighting may help young boys especially, in their emotional and physical development. In other research, a group of three- to ten-year-old girls who had been exposed to high levels of male hormones during

Conforming to type
Despite enjoying a choice of toys, children often revert to stereotypes – so a girl might ditch a "boy toy", such as a train, for a more "girly toy", such as a doll.

I've found a baby smaller than me!

Hang on, these wheels seem pretty good too...

pregnancy preferred boys' toys when compared with their sisters who were exposed to more normal levels.

Playing and learning go hand-in-hand, and the type of play that children enjoy may influence how they develop. Studies suggest that the toys children are exposed to may affect their career choices, as well as attitudes towards the opposite sex and to themselves. Most experts agree that a wide range of toys helps children develop in a balanced way, and meet their full potential as adults.

BLUE FOR BOYS, PINK FOR GIRLS?

Despite the strongly enforced colour stereotypes for boys and girls of today, a century ago in Western Europe and North America, it was pink for boys and blue for girls. Pink, as a tint of red, was thought to be a stronger colour – more suited to boys; while daintier blue was better suited to girls. Blue for girls also reflected a feminine association with the Virgin Mary. It was only after World War II that the reverse trend began.

Suiting the mood
Access to a range of toys helps a baby's development. At times, trucks and diggers fit the bill, other times a quiet moment with a teddy is best.

I wonder if I can manage to take this apart?

Hello dog. I'm tired and I think I need a cuddle.

Brothers and sisters

Are first-born children more reliable, and later ones more easy-going? While it all depends on the individual, there's some evidence that family position does have an effect on a baby's developing personality.

WHEN THERE'S A NEW BABY in the family, it's natural for older siblings to feel some pangs of jealousy over the attention being lavished on the new arrival. But even once things have settled down, the family environment will have changed for everyone. So how does a baby's birth order – where she ranks in age in relation to siblings – affect the person she will become?

FAMILY DYNAMIC

The idea that birth order may be one of the key influences that moulds a child is still a controversial one, although it has been around a while: it was first suggested by Austrian psychologist Alfred Adler, a contemporary of Sigmund Freud. One obvious reason for this influence may of course be the difference in the amount of time that parents spend with their children. When a younger sibling comes along, the older child will have already had at least a year of one-to-one time with her parents – a second child will not have this same opportunity.

Siblings also shape each other in important ways. Often, they develop different interests within a family so they are not in direct competition. For example, one sibling might excel at music, and another at sport. Perhaps surprisingly, some studies suggest that siblings closest to each other in age are the most likely to be very different from each other.

> Firstborns are typically high-achieving, conscientious, and reliable – if somewhat conservative.

BEST TO BE THE YOUNGEST?

Younger-born children are typically thought to be more adventurous, easy-going, and sociable, though perhaps a little less responsible compared with older siblings. They may also be more creative and rebellious, and inclined to be more daring. A recent US study found that younger-born adults were also more likely to take part in "dangerous" sports, such as American football, skydiving, and bobsledding.

OR THE OLDEST?

In contrast, some psychologists believe that firstborns are typically high-achieving, conscientious, and reliable – if somewhat conservative. Older-born children may also be very slightly smarter than younger siblings, according to a recent study in Norwegian military recruits. This showed that firstborn sons were on average 2.3 IQ points smarter than second-born sons, who, in turn, had slightly higher IQs than third-born sons.

So, why might this happen? In part, it may be down to the unique parental time that's lavished upon an eldest child before the birth of other siblings. But there are suggestions that firstborns will often act as "surrogate" parents to younger brothers and sisters, and that this also helps to hone their own IQs as they "tutor" little ones in the ways of life.

SIBLING ORDER

Although every child is an individual and will not necessarily conform to type, certain characteristics have been cited as being typical to children in accordance with where they fall in the family birth order.

PLAY THE FOOL

Youngest children can sometimes seem to be natural-born comedians. Because they are lower in the family pecking order, youngest children may use charm and humour to win their battles.

Younger siblings A daredevil and adventurous attitude is seen as typical of youngest siblings.

Astronauts are often cited as paragons of firstborn achievement: 21 of the first 23 NASA astronauts were either eldest children or only children.

Middle children Often a strong emphasis is placed on friendships by children who fall in the middle.

LIKE GOES WITH LIKE

A person's birth order may even influence who they end up marrying. Firstborns tend to get together with firstborns, middle children with middle children, and youngests with youngests.

GOING SOLO

Only children are in a privileged position of never having to compete for their parents' attention. Some psychologists believe that only children therefore share many of the characteristics of eldest children.

Oldest children This position often comes with a sense of responsibility that isn't replicated in younger siblings.

BIG BROTHERS

A recent study in New Zealand suggests that eldest-born sons are likely to be a full stone heavier than younger siblings as adults. Other research suggests that eldest children also tend to be taller in adulthood than younger siblings. A study of Swedish conscripts found that older brothers were slightly taller than second-born brothers, who in turn were taller than third-born brothers.

TAKE YOUR CHANCES

In many cultures, parents have historically invested much more in their firstborn sons. As far back as the Middle Ages, a system of inheritance in Europe that left everything to the eldest son meant that landless younger sons often had to be more adventurous by going off on distant military campaigns to win the spoils of war – or find a living by joining the clergy.

KEEPING THE FAITH

In immigrant families, parents may put pressure on the eldest child to uphold social and cultural values – and this may shape them differently to siblings. A study of second-generation Japanese-Americans showed that firstborn and only children (especially boys) were most likely to hold onto their Japanese culture in adulthood – living in Japanese areas, speaking Japanese, and keeping their Buddhist or Shinto faiths.

... OR STUCK IN THE MIDDLE?

Being a middle child also has its downside, as there is never a phase when they have their parents to themselves. Some experts speculate on a "middle child syndrome": the idea that some middle children may feel neglected and suffer low self-esteem, which can lead to attention-seeking behaviour. But a more positive suggestion is that middle children are uniquely placed in the family to become skilled negotiators.

Middle-born children are often thought to be great team players, and to be very sociable. Because they may not receive the special parental limelight that a firstborn or a youngest gets, they may put more of their efforts into building strong friendships outside the family.

> A 2003 study found that middle borns are the most faithful birth order – being least likely to cheat on their long-term romantic partner in adulthood.

Studies suggest that middle-born adults do indeed place a stronger value on friendships than first- or last-borns. And an Israeli study concluded that middles are like type O blood, and fit well with everyone.

But there are many factors that mould a child, and many siblings will not fit these patterns at all. Whatever the case, parents can help oldest children by not overburdening them with responsibilities, and help the youngest by resisting the urge to pamper the "baby of the family" and thus encourage their independence. In a loving family, small niggles of sibling rivalry are part and parcel of growing up, and – in the vast majority of cases – will also be accompanied by love and friendship.

66 *Before we can judge a human being, we must know the situation in which he grew up. An important moment is the position which a child occupied in his family constellation.* 99

Alfred Adler (1870–1937)

Someone to look up to
Imitating big sister

DISCOVERING THE SCIENCE

IN THIS GAME Melisa is intrigued by Helin putting a hat on her head. She spots the other hat and lifts it up to examine

HELIN AGAIN shows Melisa how to put on the hat, persevering with her demonstration, even though she finds the

Babies love to copy their older siblings' actions and behaviour.
Older children are invaluable in teaching their younger brothers
and sisters how to do things for themselves.

it carefully. She sees Helin wearing her hat, but doesn't attempt to put on her own at this stage.

task difficult. Melisa begins to get the idea – nearly there. Finally, the hat is in place, even if it needs some help to keep it on!

Left or right?

One of the ways in which our individuality shows itself is choosing to use one hand (or eye, or foot!) more than the other. How does a baby come to be right- or left-handed?

SOME TIME AROUND 18 months old, most babies start to prefer using one hand rather than the other. In around 90 per cent, this "dominant" hand will be their right one. There's even some evidence that the choice of the dominant hand develops very early on, possibly even while in the womb. Yet what actually rules hand choice – how it's determined, and what it means in terms of how our brains work – is still the subject of debate.

DIFFERENT SIDES

The large top part of the brain, the cortex, consists of two hemispheres – left and right – which are joined by a bundle of nerve fibres. But there is an odd crossover between brain and body: the muscles on the right side of the body are controlled by the left hemisphere, and vice versa.

Each of the hemispheres is specialized to some degree for particular tasks. The best example of this is language processing, which is usually carried out in the left hemisphere. However, in a small percentage of people, language is dealt with by the right. The chance of having this unusual setup depends on which hand is dominant: it's found in nearly one in three left-handed people, but only one in twenty right-handed people.

As a baby grows, the brain establishes its neural pathways. Left-handed children tend to have more complicated pathways and neurological patterns. This may be because the left bias is not complete. They could be left-handed, but have the right foot dominant, for example.

ESTABLISHING DOMINANCE

In practice, for the first year or more of their lives, babies are largely ambidextrous. There are some ways to tell which hand may become dominant, usually by seeing which hand they choose to reach for toys in front of them, or which hand they use to feed themselves. This isn't hard and fast, though – and indeed, if they favour one hand all the time, paediatricians would be concerned that this may point to some kind of problem that is stopping them from using the other hand.

IS THERE A LEFT-HANDED GENE?

Which hand is dominant appears to be an inherited characteristic to some extent: but the exact gene or genes associated with this are still unclear. What is known is that boys are slightly more likely to be left-handed than girls – at 11.6 per cent of boys versus 8.6 per cent of girls. One study has found that a higher birth weight seems to point to future right-handedness in boys and left-handedness in girls.

chances of having a left-handed child

2 right-handed parents

ARE WE LEFT-BRAINED OR RIGHT-BRAINED?

There's a popular idea that people are either "left-brained" or "right-brained", and that babies grow up to be one or the other. So-called left-brainers are allegedly logical, planning types because the calculation and language half of the brain is supposedly more dominant. Right-brainers, by contrast, are said to be more free-thinking, artistic, and creative. But most neuroscientists have always found this is a very crude division, and successive studies have debunked it. In other words, a baby's future path isn't determined by neural hard-wiring on one side or the other – they can be organized and creative at the same time.

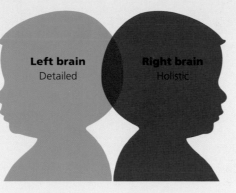

Left brain
Detailed

Right brain
Holistic

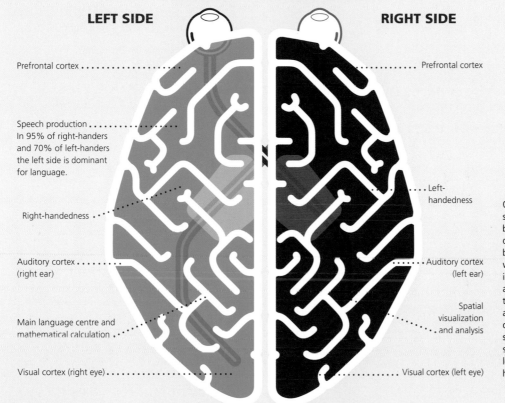

LEFT SIDE

RIGHT SIDE

Prefrontal cortex

Prefrontal cortex

Speech production
In 95% of right-handers and 70% of left-handers the left side is dominant for language.

Left-handedness

Right-handedness

Auditory cortex
(right ear)

Auditory cortex
(left ear)

Main language centre and mathematical calculation

Spatial visualization and analysis

Visual cortex (right eye)

Visual cortex (left eye)

Our brains are cross-wired so that one side of the brain controls functions on the other side of the body. This is true of our vision and hearing, where inputs from the right eye and ear are processed on the left side of the brain, and vice-versa. Some other functions, such as speech processing and spatial awareness, are located in a particular hemisphere.

chances of having a left-handed child

1 right- and 1 left-handed parent

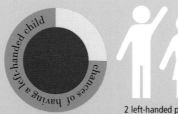

chances of having a left-handed child

2 left-handed parents

Just being me

By their first birthday, babies are emerging as little people
with their own likes, dislikes, and characteristics.
But how much of this is determined from birth – or even before?

MANY PARENTS think they can recognize aspects of their baby's characteristics and temperament from the beginning. Others expect their baby's personality to be formed by whatever events and environments she encounters in life. Researchers are looking at both elements – because, undoubtedly, people brought up in similar environments may still react to those environments in different ways. And, from the beginning, babies do appear to have different interests and styles of behaviour – even in things as minor as whether a four-month-old is fascinated by her feet, or a nine-month old appears to be shyer than her twin sister. So, just how ingrained is a baby's personality?

EMERGING PERSONALITY

Some experts believe that a baby's personality starts to be distinguishable in the first weeks of life, and that by as early as three or four months some of her tendencies are quite clear. For instance, small babies who are tense and irritable when introduced to new objects are more prone to be shy and nervous later in childhood and adolescence.

Other research takes a more biological approach, looking at how the neurotransmitter chemicals in the brain appear to affect personality by regulating moods and responses. In particular, researchers have looked at the connections between dopamine and serotonin

{ Shyness is a trait that babies start to develop only from around six months old. }

genes, and a child's tendency towards anger and frustration. While such factors are likely to be present from birth, other aspects of personality may be shaped even earlier, by pre-birth experiences – for example, excessive stress in a pregnant mother is believed to have an adverse effect on the baby.

NURTURE VERSUS NATURE

But even given the influences that are present early on, a baby's personality will still develop over time, depending on her experiences. One very important factor is, of course, the parenting a baby receives. Parents who exercise control gently, allowing children to follow their own ideas and goals as far as possible, are encouraging them to be more motivated and to regulate their own behaviour – and, eventually, to develop the personality traits that will help them to control their own lives.

Overall, temperament appears to be influenced by all sorts of factors, from the biological to the social. And inevitably, parents will continue to feel they understand their babies completely – or to be utterly baffled by them. Or fall somewhere in between. Personality and temperament are, after all, the things that make us who we are. It may be that we can never know, exactly, what shapes personality, because that would be to unpick what it means to be the unique individuals that we are.

Little baby, big personality

Some experts place babies' personalities into three broad types, but most children are usually a mixture of all three:

EASY OR HAPPY
Active, tolerate change, don't anger easily, often like new people and situations.

SHY/SLOW TO WARM
Sensitive to surroundings, resistant to change, need time to transition between activities.

SPIRITED
Strong-willed, active and impulsive, defiant, intense, in need of firm structure.

Child of her time

There's no crystal ball to look into the future and see what a child may become. But, predictions do suggest that today's babies will hopefully be blessed with longer and healthier lives than previous generations.

THE LAST FEW DECADES have seen major strides in the health of children and adults around the world. This is true even in developed countries like the US and the UK, where huge health gains had already been made in the 20th century, and continue into the 21st century.

For children born in the decade 2010 the world over, the good news is that, on average, they will probably live much longer than their parents. According to predictions from the UK's Office for National Statistics, girls born in the UK in 2013 can expect to live on average to 83, but, if future advances in medicine and technology are taken into account, this could rise to 94; for a boy the figure would be 90 (compared to 79 expected today) although this gender gap is closer in more affluent areas. Overall, if health improvements continue, one-third of this generation could reach 100 years of age. When these children reach their mid-60s, their lives may be very different from those of elderly people living today. Many of their friends will also still be healthy and active, so they are likely to be surrounded by youthful peers into old age. However, with falling fertility rates worldwide, there may be fewer young people to support this age group, and they'll have to work for longer. While this generation will also face other challenges, such as climate change, scientific advances that may help deal with such problems are expected to continue apace in the 21st century.

LOOKING AHEAD

Switching off the TV and spending time outdoors may be good for babies' eyesight, according to a major study that has been tracking children in the UK since the 1990s. Around **25–50% of UK children** will become **short-sighted** and need glasses as young adults, while in parts of **southeast Asia**, this rises to **80%.** Children who spent more time outdoors at age eight were half as likely to be short-sighted by 15, the study found.

CROWDED EARTH

The world population was **7.2 billion in mid-2013.** UN predictions suggest it will reach a massive **9.6 billion by 2050,** and then **10.9 billion by 2100.** The number of **over-60s** is projected to rise from **841 million in 2013** to **2 billion by 2050.**

{ *If health improvements continue, one-third of this generation could reach* **100 years** *of age.* }

Generation gap Melisa's grandmother looks fit and healthy. Her genes should be a good legacy for Melisa for a healthy future.

GLOBAL CHILD

Figures from the World Health Organization indicate that a **"global girl"** born in **2012** has a current life expectancy of **73 years**, and a **"global boy"** can expect to live for **68 years.** This is six years more than that predicted for a child born in 1990. The **gains in life expectancy** have been greatest in poorer countries. Children born in high-income countries are still expected to live the longest.

NEXT GENERATION

Will baby girls born in **2012** go on to have babies themselves? Possibly, possibly not – across the world, **fertility rates are falling**. One in five **women aged 45** in the **UK in 2011** was childless, and many women are now choosing not to have children; especially in the UK, Singapore, and the US.

" *While this generation will also face other challenges, such as climate change, scientific advances that may help deal with such problems are expected to continue apace in the 21st century.* "

HAPPY FIRST BIRTHDAY MELISA

What lies behind us and what lies ahead of us are tiny matters compared to what lives within us

Henry David Thoreau
(1817–1862)
US philosopher

Index

Acknowledgements

Dorling Kindersley would like to thank the following people for their contribution to *Watch My Baby Grow*:

Particular thanks are due to the consultant editor and writer, **Susan Watt**, who is a science writer and editor. She has developed books for major publishers including BBC Worldwide and Dorling Kindersley. She has one son and lives in London and Derbyshire, UK.

Grateful thanks to **Babylab at Birkbeck, University of London,** for agreeing to be associated with this project. The Centre for Brain and Cognitive Development (CBDB) is part of Birkbeck University, and is internationally recognized as a centre of academic excellence.

Special thanks to **Dr Victoria Southgate, Babylab at Birkbeck,** for her considerable contribution to the text, as well as for her work as a consultant.

Thanks also to **Dr Teodora Gliga**, **Babylab at Birkbeck,** for additional writing work and consultancy.

Shaoni Bhattacharya is an award-winning freelance journalist who has contributed to three other DK pregnancy titles. She is a consultant for *New Scientist* magazine. She lives with her husband, son and daughter in London, UK.

Radhika Holmstrom is a journalist who writes about parenting and health for readers ranging from doctors to first-time parents. She lives in London and has two daughters of her own.

Sally J Hall has been a parenting journalist for many years, working on major UK magazines including *Mother & Baby* and *Pregnancy & Birth*. She has two children and lives in London.

Emma Young is an award-winning health and science journalist. She has worked on *The Guardian* and the *Sydney Morning Herald*. With two young children, Emma now freelances from her home in Sheffield, UK.

Niki Foreman is a writer, editor, and mum to baby Joshua. She was an editor at DK in London for seven years before moving to Sydney, where she now writes and edits a variety of books for publishers around the globe.

Other contributors: Anna Pollard, Ben Morgan, and Clare Sansom.

Dorling Kindersley would also like to thank the following:
Additional design Charlotte Bull and Lucy Parissi
Anatomical illustrations Patrick Mulrey
All other illustrations Philip Gilderdale at Project 360
Indexer Marie Lorimer
Additional baby models: Romilly Martin, Jayden Chui from Scallywags, and Leo Flynn
Hair and make-up Anna Durston
Photographer's assistant Jenny Patterson

Every effort has been made to ensure that the information in this book is complete and accurate. However, neither the publisher nor the authors are engaged in rendering professional advice or services to the individual reader. The contents of this book are not intended as a substitute for consulting with your healthcare provider. All matters regarding the health of your baby require medical supervision. Neither the publisher nor the authors shall be liable or responsible for any loss or damage allegedly arising from any information and suggestions in this book.

New photography by Ruth Jenkinson.
All other images © Dorling Kindersley
For further information, see www.dkimages.com

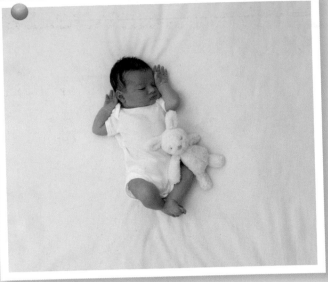
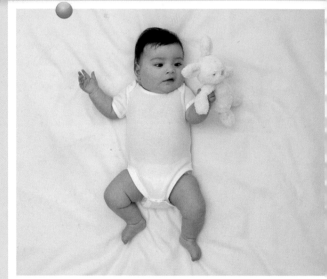
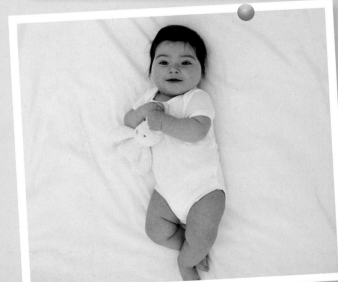